Awareness

Awareness

by
Eileen J. Garrett

With a Foreword by Rhea A. White

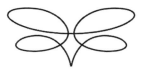

Helix Press
New York

Published by Helix Press
An imprint of the
Parapsychology Foundation, Inc.
PO Box 1562
New York, New York, 10021, USA

TEL: 212-628-1550 / FAX: 212-628-1559

Printed by
BookMasters, Inc.
Ashland, Ohio, USA

Cover art designed by
Illuminations, Inc.
Greenport, New York, USA

ISBN 10:1-931747-22-9
ISBN 13: 978-1-931747-22-6

Table of Contents

Prologue

As the granddaughter of Eileen J. Garrett, author of *Awareness* I realize full well that she was a highly complex individual who during her lifetime—she was born in 1893 and died in 1970—was an author, lecturer, entrepreneur, business executive, publisher, psychic medium and healer as well as the founder of Parapsychology Foundation, the nonprofit organization I currently administer as its Executive Director. Parapsychology Foundation acts as a worldwide forum supporting scientific exploration of psychic phenomena.

Born in Ireland and living in England until she became an American citizen in the 1940s, Eileen Garrett, all her life, possessed mediumistic faculties. These so-called gifts included telepathy, clairvoyance, clairaudience, trance mediumship as well as an ability to diagnose illness in a clairvoyant manner, but always in consultation with physicians and psychologists. She was the author of non-fiction books addressing psychic matters including her cogent autobiography, *Adventures in the Supernormal,* recently brought back into print and available through the Foundation's imprint, Helix Press. She wrote three works of fiction under the *nom de plume* of Jeanne Lyttle, edited various anthologies in the field of psychic research and published the reknown quarterly review of psychic research, *Tomorrow Magazine* as well as the scholarly *International Journal of Parapsychology* that the Foundation is once again proud to publish. Convinced that the study of psychic matters was best served by consideration by many disciplines and as truly an international pursuit, she sponsored many international conferences devoted to parapsychology welcoming academicians and scientists to join in a concentrated effort to find answers to the questions raised by psychic functioning.

My mother, Eileen Coly, Garrett's daughter and current President of Parapsychology Foundation, and I, when asked to try to describe the force of her personality and her beliefs, refer to her own ability to set pen to paper and freely and lucidly organize her own thoughts and experiences in the psychic world which speak eloquently for the Lady herself.

Eileen Coly and I are most grateful that the late Dr. Rhea A. White, our esteemed colleague and long-time PF associate, grantee, author and conference participant not to mention valued personal friend, had graciously shared her comments on and consideration of Garrett's *Awareness* manuscript for this volume. Grace to her far-reaching and meticulous career, Rhea with her many resources coupled with a personal first-hand knowledge of Eileen J. Garrett, was eminently suited to contribute her reflections of *Awareness,* for which we are most appreciative.

I am very proud to share with you what I feel to be an extraordinary document of value to humankind. *Awareness* was written and first published within the crucible of The Second World War in 1943 and then again reprinted with a subsequent Preface by Garrett to the Second Edition released in the 1960s.

I would caution that some of the material presented refers obviously to a bygone era but her message remains current, as we lamentably seem to have learned little over the intervening years, mired as we are in unpredictable, hostile and dangerous world events.

We may surely benefit from the timeless message of *Awareness* ... a plea for a new evolution of the individual life as envisioned by Eileen J. Garrett.

Lisette Coly
Executive Director
Parapsychology Foundation
New York, March 2007

Foreword

Before Reading *Awareness* Again
After Fifty Years

I read several books by Eileen Garrett when I was at the Parapsychology Laboratory at Duke University in the 1950s. I was enthralled by her books, not for their "oh wow" value, although there was an element of that. She was a medium of great reknown in the U.S., the U.K., and indeed, throughout the world!

It was not only the subject matter (facets of her life as a psychic and medium, which she described), but she was a "mover and shaker" in regard to promoting parapsychology as a science. She initiated the Parapsychology Foundation which, since its beginning in the 1950s, has been the leader in bringing together parapsychologists from around the world and scholars from many disciplines. This has greatly broadened and deepened the field and extended its geographic and interdisciplinary boundaries.

The Foundation accomplishes this in several ways: through its international conferences and their published proceedings; through Garrett's books, editorials, and articles; through the Foundation's newsletter and journal; and by giving research and travel grants to researchers, providing financial support for college students interested in parapsychology, and holding lectures open to the public.

Mrs. Garrett, as she was usually referred to, has written some of the best books available about what it feels like to be a psychic and a medium and the far-reaching implications of both. *Awareness* is one of the best. In rereading this book after fifty years, I was not only greatly impressed all over again after all those years in the field, but I saw more clearly than when I was a newcomer the great value it has for persons who have had any kind of exceptional experience, not only psychic ones. I will elaborate on this in the Afterword at the end of this book.

I also sometimes wondered, as the years passed and I became a seasoned parapsychologist, whether my high regard for Mrs. Garrett may have been partly due to the fact that I had read her books and editorials when I was new to the field. After reading it recently, I now know that *was* the case. She conveys firsthand knowledge of what it is like to be a psychic and medium better than any one I have read.

I had the privilege of knowing Mrs. Garrett, who could be intimidating on occasion, but who was always interesting. Through her books, articles, and editorials, the knowledge she imparted is still as important for 21st-century readers, including myself, even as it was in the 1950s. In fact, with age and experience, I have come to understand what she wrote and recognize its importance more fully on this later reading than when I was new to the field.

I'm confident that those who read this and others of her several books will agree. Her overmastering personality is matched by her wisdom concerning the "inside" of being psychic because she was so highly aware and conscious of the process involved from her own personal experience. It didn't hurt that she was such a good writer that she was able to convey the details of her life and experiences such that the reader feels "inside her head."

Awareness should open inner doors for anyone who reads it, whether it is the first or a subsequent reading.

Rhea A. White
New Bern, North Carolina
November 2006

Preface to the First Edition

I have decided to publish this book this year because the pressure of world events and the tension of the times have created an extraordinary sensitiveness in the consciousness of millions of men and women, and because this sensitiveness is increasingly being expressed in various forms of inquiry. These inquiries are concerned with the nature and quality of the subtle forces that are operating in the world and affecting the destinies of individuals and nations; they are concerned with the causes and meanings of "psychic" episodes that are being experienced both in the impersonal concentrations of battle, by men in the armed forces, and by the lay populations in their long and selfless waiting upon the development of events.

These are times of great change, and many people are looking out on the swiftly moving sequence of readjustments in an aborted attempt to discover the source, the nature, and the meaning of the world upheaval. Yet in the long, slow processes of evolution, civilization is the only thing which has changed in any perceptible measure; the current conflict is a man-made condition; and our understanding of its meaning is to be clarified only through a fresh and fuller awareness of our own potentialities and of the effects we create in using them, or in failing to use them. The present climax is a tension which has been evolved by the human consciousness. And we are facing the prospect of a new world because humanity has prepared itself for a more ample way of living, for life more abundant. The seeds of this new amplitude are not planted anywhere in the world outside ourselves, but deep in the nature and the consciousness of mankind.

From my personal point of view, the book has a double purpose. In the first place, it is the result of the re-examination of the field of my own faith. As many people already know, this faith is not simply a theoretical or philosophical structure, but is the cumulative effect, to date, of my life experience. It has been critically examined by me, and as will be clear in the following pages, it has been submitted to testing in the scientific field. But science, with all its undeniable splendors of achievement, is restricted by its self-imposed limitations to the field of after-the-fact. It deals with the "given," but excludes the source of the gift. Yet only in the psychological capacities of mankind can the actual significance of events be conceived, accepted, and lived by; and it is out of this same area that the capacities of science—its curiosity, its persistence, its judgment, and its inspiration—emerge. Humanity is itself the laboratory and testing ground of all possible events in the universe; and we are now living through an important phase of our endless experience of testing. In this book I invite your attention beyond the field of the "given," into areas where the giving occurs; and I have endeavored to indicate, without dogmatism, some aspects of my own experience in the subtle perceptive testing of that sphere.

The second purpose of the book is to furnish a response—some measure of assurance—to the widespread sensitivity to which I have referred. It is to encourage, without pressure, and to justify, as far as it may, the sense of reality in the intuitional and supersensory experiences of the times. The education of most of us has been dominated by modern emphasis upon substance, "reality," and the senses. But deep in the structure and quality of human nature there reside supersensory capacities, known of old but temporarily neglected, by means of which man is capable of achieving knowledge of the immaterial world, capable of perceiving events that occur in space-time far beyond the reach which science claims for the senses.

This immaterial field of human perception is as factual to awareness and as real to life as the field of substance, and we are constantly brushing the edges of its reality in our intuitions, our day-dreams, and our creative inspirations. All of these constitute the fringes of supersensory perception, though for the most part they occur outside the areas of our awareness. We have not been adequately taught how to grasp these gossamer filaments of the future which, tomorrow, will be the present; nevertheless the human consciousness is becoming aware of itself and of its affinities throughout the universe. The visions, apparitions, premonitions, and other super-sensory manifestations of being, which men and women experience in times of impersonal tension and uplift, are factually true in consciousness—echoes which reach us from the fertile hills of heaven, when we are ourselves somewhat universalized, lights reflected from waves on the mysterious sea of the whole of life.

I am deeply impressed by this present moment in evolution. It is a time of man's return to himself, of humanity's reconcentration of attention upon itself. Rather abruptly we are coming to see that all the distresses that have harassed human nature in the current century are of man's own making. In a fair field of possibilities in which we were free to make whatever we chose, we have failed to fulfill the desire of the human heart; and we all inescapably face the fact that what we have made is not good enough to satisfy human nature in its present phase of development.

Human nature thus becomes the critic of all current forms of civilization. And seeing how, on every hand, nature continues to swing through her established cycles without suffering the pains that we endure, we turn once more to listen to the voice of our own nature—which alone, of all created things upon this earth, knows the difference between the agonies of conflict, pain, and want and the joy of its own normal fulfillment.

We are all seeking such natural fulfillments, consciously and unconsciously. And there are countless evidences which indicate that the human race now stands at the threshold of a new and universalistic illumination. But to be adequately effective in human life, this fresh light must be freely accepted by the consciousness of mankind. We must become aware of it as true and real, though it shines in regions that lie beyond the reach of the senses. It must be perceived and recognized as the single universal light, and we must know, individually and collectively, that all its apparent differentiations occur only through our failure to perceive it clearly, or through our willful resistance to its penetration. Realizing—as one trusts we inevitably shall—that the darkness so deeply enveloping humanity is caused by no failure in the light, but is a shadow cast by man himself and impeding the vital radiance, we shall move to allow the light to dissipate that shadow and freely nourish the fruits of peace, justice, and freedom throughout the civilized world.

It has been suggested that this book strikes a rather "religious" note. To my sense, however, this suggestion expresses the very essence of the difficulty of the times. Certainly the book is not "religious" in any dogmatic or sectarian sense. The primal energy that operates throughout the universe is a single unified power, and all of our concentrations upon the countless different forms in which we perceive it are, in fact, attempts to penetrate to the realization of its unity.

Religion is not a separate compartment of human life, not something mysterious and unknowable and cut off from the "practical" experiences of our daily work and from scientific experimentation. One of the most significant facts of our era is that psychology has dared to enter the list of the sciences. In this event science and religion and art and the every-day activities of all of us come to a focus at the level of basic values. Psychology will become the lens through which the diffused and many-colored lights of life will be re-fused, for our perception and understanding, into a primal unity. There will always be a religious field, for it is the nature of man to aspire, and the areas of the unknown are infinite. But the areas of the unknown are also the field of science, as they are the little domains in which our individual curiosity finds its problems, our little experiences find solutions and significance. All of human life is the quest of consciousness to identify itself with itself, through understanding. The human consciousness is forever a pioneer; religion and science are both phases of its endless search—phases of the spiritual adventure of man among all the manifestations of vitality that occur in the universe.

Curiosity, courage, experience, understanding—these are the steps in the ever-rising development of individual lives and of the human consciousness as a whole. Science seeks to discover the established, the repeatedly demonstrable, and religion seeks to serve and sustain the basic laws and truths of being, even those which are incomprehensible to our finite abilities. And between these two broad racial highways the individual follows a middle path, each one according to his ability and his talent, seeking and finding his own measure of truth, receiving and reflecting the light of life according to his capacity and his need.

My fate, my life, have largely consisted in experiencing the tenuous, the rare, the unique event in awareness. Of my own volition I have pressed consciousness toward the limits of its present phase.

According to my capacity to do so, I have knocked at doors of the supersensory house of life, and they have opened to me responsively. My faith in the "unknowable" has been established by my experience in the "unknown"; and I record this faith and this experience as an act of service to a distraught world, so that those who are ready—and there are many of these—may be encouraged to accept into their field of awareness those seeds of intuition and supersensory perception which are now so commonly allowed to fall on the barren ground of inattention or on the stony places of rationalism.

I know very well, of and for my own knowledge, that beyond the doors which have opened to me there are countless other doors which I have not yet approached. I have a deep and abiding faith in the future of mankind; but the human consciousness can know only what it perceives, and only by adequately understanding what we have already experienced can we progress. There are no known limits to the field of the human consciousness; its capacities transcend both the phase of substance and the reach of the senses; it has affinities with the universal. Ever and always, the human consciousness possesses its own standards and measures of reality, and I have given this book *Awareness* as a title because awareness is the strange and subtle bridge which leads consciousness from faith to knowledge, from intimation to understanding. Over this bridge we move toward all individual creativeness, through ever fuller identification of the parts with the whole.

For me, the book is an episode in service, a gift to the future. It is a symbol of my faith in myself, in humanity as a whole, and in the spiritual bases of the universe. It is a declaration in behalf of the indivisible unity of life, with which it deals; for I have seen how knowledge of the immaterial fields of being, supersensorily perceived and translated for awareness, has been developed into substance and form and action in the physical world. I know that beyond the restricted areas of our common interests we are all potentially capable of a relative greatness; and learning, as I do learn, of the courage, fortitude, and endurance of millions of human beings everywhere, and of the heroic superconscious achievements of men in their moments of depersonalized activity under the stress of battle of whatever disaster, I am moved to offer the assurances of these few pages, in order that men may be encouraged to accept their intimations of immortality and their dreams of more abundant living.

These activities in consciousness are not illusions, but foreshadowings of the future toward which we are so swiftly moving—which we are already experiencing, in fact, in our more subtle sensitivities. In our own field, and by virtue of our own nature, we are active collaborators with the creative principle in the universe; and as we become identified with it, we expand both our nature and our field of life.

My own life is built and operates on these levels of faith and practice. Though made up of many parts, it is unified through faith and understanding. I know that the individual consciousness, cultivated and developed beyond the sensory field, increases the perceptive capacity of the senses; that all phases of the finite are dependent upon the universal; that the sources of inspiration exist beyond materiality and individualism. I shall continue to knock at the still-hidden doors of the infinite as I succeed in discovering them; and to the best of my ability, I shall continue—as in the past—to set awareness free in the supersensory and superpersonal fields of consciousness, and to move impartially in the detailed relationships of practical work and living as well.

Eileen J. Garrett
New York City
September 1943

Preface to the Second Edition

I have just reexamined this volume, some two decades after it was originally written, and I must confess to being somewhat startled by the impression which this examination has made on me. To begin with, the words I used in the original Preface, written in the midst of the Second World War, have a shockingly timely ring in this period of new East-West tensions, abortive summit meetings and missile tests; once again, it is eminently appropriate to speak of "the pressure of world events and the tension of the times ..."

Much, of course, has actually happened during the years that have passed to enlarge the awareness to psychic phenomena among the general public and within the scientific community. A decade after the original publication of this volume, it was my privilege, as President of the Parapsychology Foundation, Inc., to welcome scientists from many parts of the world to the First International Conference of Parapsychological Studies at the University of Utrecht, the Netherlands, in 1953. During the years that followed, I was able to devote much of my work to the examination of psychic manifestations within a scientific framework. I was thus able to move out of myself, and into wider areas of activity, where I could be the subject of scholarly inquiry into my own work as a sensitive, as well as part of an organized effort to enlarge the horizons of scientific research in such areas as physics, psychology, biochemistry, electrobiology and pharmacology.

As I write these lines, I have just returned to the European Regional Headquarters of the Parapsychology Foundation, following orientation trips through Canada, parts of the United States and several countries of Western Europe. I am much encouraged to see that serious scholarly studies into the marvels and mysteries of the human mind are making considerable strides, and that the challenge of parapsychology is being met by an increasing number of distinguished scientists.

There is a French saying that "The more things change, the more they remain the same." Looking at the day's newspaper headlines, one is tempted to agree that this is, indeed, so. Happily, however, parapsychological studies have not stood still during the two decades that have almost past since this book was originally written; and I am humbly proud of having been able to contribute my share to this progress.

                                                    Eileen J. Garrett
                                            Le Piol, St. Paul de Vence
                                                      France, 1963

I
Consciousness

THERE IS A PHILOSOPHY which holds that consciousness, like energy, is ubiquitous, and that each individual unit of being in existence partakes of the universal consciousness as it partakes of the universal energy, according to its particular nature and constitution.

The nature and the consciousness of a thing are inseparable, the capacities of its consciousness being the measure of its nature. Thus, in the scheme of things as they are, the relationships of any given unit of life are precisely limited by its nature, while its nature is revealed by its capacity for relationships—the possible field of activity of its consciousness.

A block of granite, a wild flower, an oak tree, a bee, a dog, or a man has each its own individual nature and its own particular capacity for relationships with other things in the world, each of these other things being also endowed with a particular nature, measure of consciousness, and capacity for relationships.

When we come to consider human nature and the human consciousness we enter a field so subtle, so complex, and so extensive that modern psychology is just beginning to grasp some of its more obvious aspects, and finds itself completely confused before certain relational activities that are possible to the consciousness of man. Among these activities are telepathy, clairvoyance, trance, and all mediumistic phenomena. But what happens to consciousness in the normal sleep of all men and women is also not understood by psychology.

In undertaking to write about the human consciousness, therefore, one enters a field which is both confused and mysterious. Yet if one possesses capacities that do operate in the more mysterious areas of this field, a recording of the direct knowledge gained in the activities of these capacities may help to clarify the confusion.

My own belief is that the whole field in which the human consciousness operates may be divided into three principal parts which correspond to those three divisions of time that we call the past, the present, and the future. But this division of the consciousness is arbitrary. It is simply a convenient method of analysis that we adopt to assist our further understanding of the problem by relating it to what we already understand. Actually, the field in which the human consciousness operates is a complete and indi-

1

visible whole, like the space-time continuum which science has lately come to realize. In fact, the space-time continuum is the very field in which the human consciousness moves and perceives. This field consists of infinite and indivisible space wedded to eternal and indivisible time; and in this limitless and unified field—this continuum which is the fourth dimension of all that happens in the universe—the consciousness of mankind is free (potentially, at least) to operate, to perceive, and to record its impressions. The space-time continuum represents our conception of eternity, and we are living in eternity now.

If consciousness is thus free in space-time, why do we not all wander far afield in past and future time at will? Why do such vast areas of space, before which the human understanding pauses in awe and confusion, continue to remain mysterious?

To answer such questions is to take further steps in the analysis of consciousness; and perhaps an interesting way to do this is to recall how Professor Einstein perfected his mathematical equation of the universe.

When the relativity theory was published and the scientists began to study it, some of them asked questions that the Einstein equations failed to answer in a completely satisfactory manner. Science recognized a world in flux all about us; the relativities of relationships among things, all in motion, constituted a chaos of movement, and there was no base of stability anywhere. At the same time, many dependable laws seemed to operate in the universe, like the law of gravity and the laws of rhythmic cycles, and the scientists were convinced that somewhere there must exist a stabilizing force, still undiscovered, which somehow gave system and organization to the flux.

To solve the problem, and by means of a mathematical gesture, Dr. Einstein finally gave form to the formless universe, declaring that though it was infinite in extent it was still a unit, and that its infinite unity was the stabilizing force that dominated the whole finite flux. The influence of the unitary, all-enclosing whole maintained an everlasting equilibrium among all of the movements occurring within it. He called the stabilizing outer circumference of the universe "the macroscopic atom," and he declared its nature to be the direct opposite of the microscopic atoms, of which all the finite fluctuant things in the world are composed.

In this courageous performance, Dr. Einstein gave us a fresh key to the secrets of the human consciousness. His solution of the baffling problem of the finite flux was achieved by a creative excursion of consciousness itself— an excursion that embraced the whole universe. Mankind had always been intuitively aware of a supreme controlling law, and had thought of it vaguely as Deity or God; but Einstein's transformation of the metaphysical idea into a formula which science could understand and accept was a unique, free, and independent act of the human mind. No scientist or philosopher had previously achieved an equal dialectical completeness. The declaration of the macroscopic atom constituted a definite and dramatic expansion of the human consciousness toward an ultimate unity.

Each human being is a finite part of this conceptual whole. But most of us are pretty thoroughly occupied, consciously and actively, with our immediate rather than our remote relationships; and it is simply because of the immediacy of our usual interests that the field of our consciousness-activity is limited and curtailed. People and events that are remote from us in time and space remain remote from our interest also, and we become habituated to limited fields of attention.

We may not often recall the image of the Eiffel Tower, Rheims Cathedral, or the Taj Mahal, but we can do so at will. And if by some chance our interest in the Moon or the rings of Saturn is stirred, we can project our consciousness toward these more distant relationships. Or again, if we plan to build a house, it is possible to create the entire project, in detail, in the mind, in purpose, and on paper—no matter where the actual site of the projected structure may be—before even a shovelful of earth is dug for the foundation.

These and countless other facts (including the fact that the mind of man can and does achieve such all-inclusive concepts as the macroscopic atom) prove that the human consciousness is not necessarily bound down to the areas of diverse time and event which lie within the limited field of our sensory preception and our ordinary conscious experience. We do not go abroad more freely in the space-time continuum simply because we do not desire with sufficient intensity to do so. But we can do so if we choose.

All the finite things that together make up the tremendous flux of life in the world as we know it are individualized entities. Each has its own particular nature and its own quantum of consciousness. Its precise place in relation to the whole is fixed by these innate facts, and cannot be gainsaid. But nowhere in the three kingdoms of nature below the human kingdom does there exist any type of capacity that is comparable to the consciousness of man.

The mineral kingdom is inorganic in structure, and its consciousness is both limited in extent and purely automatic in kind. It reacts limitedly to certain effects from without, but it has no volitions.

The vegetable kingdom also exists and develops automatically, for the most part; but it possesses certain structural differentiations that may be thought of as "organic," and it exhibits certain responses to environing conditions which indicate sensitivities the mineral kingdom does not possess. But it also is non-volitional; it endures whatever happens to it without protest or means of escape.

In the animal kingdom there exist great varieties of physical development in different directions—paws, wings, and fins—with capacities for mobility in numerous conditions of time and space. These capacities for mobility mark a tremendous release from the restricted field of automatism, a tremendous expansion in consciousness potential, for they involve vast possibilities of varied experience through the mere changing of environment. Many animal types possess complex organic structure, and the animal also *feels* in a manner in which the mineral and vegetable kingdoms do not. It may be broadly said that the whole existence of the animal kingdom is closely bound to its feeling capacities, "feeling" which is based completely in individual self-reference. In the animal kingdom self-preservation is truly the first law of life. Instinct, which is the operation of this always self-referred feeling, is the normal law and rule of the animal kingdom in its natural state.

It has been said that self-preservation is the primary law of human life too. Yet history, and especially the history of the present war-torn years, reveals not only that "the right is more precious than peace," but that it is more precious than life itself. All over the world, as these words are written, millions of men and women are risking and giving their lives for collective causes which are more or less impersonal to them individually, but which they recognize as greater than themselves. After this exhibition of selfless heroism on an unprecedented world-scale, we need never again be misled into the delusion that individual self-preservation is the first law of human life. That distinction belongs to the animal kingdom. The consciousness and the nature of mankind are not focused at so low a level or on so small a scale.

Allied to that old self-preservation fallacy, there is another illusion which needs to be eliminated from our common acceptance. This is the idea that the faculty which renders man superior to the other three kingdoms in nature is his self-consciousness, his sense of his own individual existence. *Cogito ergo sum.* But egotistic self-consciousness is no longer the crown of man's uniqueness—if it ever were. On the contrary, a man whose consciousness is mainly centered in himself is limited to a field that lies very close to the levels of instinct.

The true crown of man's uniqueness lies in his capacity for impersonal objective perception; it lies in his innate ability to perceive and judge and understand the facts of objective reality independently of any thought of their direct relation to himself. The crown of man's uniqueness lies in the ability of his consciousness to transcend his own individualism.

This capacity for objective impersonal perception and appreciation, which resides in the consciousness of mankind only, may be thought of as a capacity for the abstraction of consciousness. For a thing to be abstract it must be abstracted from something. And in the abstract operations of the human consciousness, consciousness itself is abstracted from the finite fields of immediate sensory perception, and moves outward into wider measures of unity with the universal Whole.

A concept like Einstein's macroscopic atom, or the concept of an omnipotent, omnipresent, and omniscient Deity as ruling the flux of activities in the world, can be brought into man's conscious perception only by a displacement of the ordinary sensory activities of our consciousness, and by a concentration of attention upon the images that come into the field of our awareness as we strive to grasp the form, the substance, and the nature—the *meaning*—of such abstract ideas.

Let us imagine a person waking out of a long sound sleep, briefly becoming aware of himself and his environment, and then projecting his consciousness outward to grasp the reality of the macroscopic atom. We thus survey the three principal phases of the human consciousness which correspond to the three divisions of time that we commonly speak of as "the past, the present, and the future"; and we may call these three main aspects of consciousness as a whole the Subconscious, the Conscious, and the Superconscious.

The subconscious is related to the past—the inherited and experienced past of the individual. The conscious operates always in the present—in each "here" and "now" of the individual in the constantly shifting relativities of time and space. The superconscious is the field of the future and the individually unknown, the entire field of the universal that lies outside the individual's subconscious and conscious fields, no matter whether the data of this superconscious field exist in the past, the present, or the future areas of our divided conception of time. This is the supersensory field, a field in which perception does not depend on the five senses. Into this super-sensory field the abstract consciousness of the human being is capable of expanding.

This is a drastic statement; for it is generally supposed that man's five senses are the messengers and agents of the human consciousness in its relations with the world that lies outside itself. And so they are. By the means of hearing, seeing, tasting, smelling, and touching countless things in the outer world, we become aware of their various natures and qualities. But science has held that the senses are the *only* means by which the human consciousness can become aware of the objective world. Yet the human mind, by virtue of its innate capacities, has discovered a world that is vastly different from and immensely greater than the world which we know by way of the five senses.

For example, science has discovered that, both above and below the range of human hearing, there exist areas of sound vibration which the human ear does not hear. Similarly, both above and below the range of all we ever see there exist areas of light vibration to which the human eye does not react.

Consequently, in addition to the three main phases of consciousness that we have already mentioned we must also consider the peculiar nature of awareness. Awareness is a faculty of the mind, by means of which *attention* may be variously directed, at will, into particular phases of the past, the present, or the future. Generally speaking, any present awareness represents a concentration of attention, in some degree, upon the content of one of our three divisions of consciousness. And usually, this involves the activity of one or more of the five senses.

But there are certain concentrations of consciousness in which awareness is withdrawn as far as possible from the impact of all sensory perceptions, and in which attention is focused within the organism as a relatively isolated unit of life, alienated as completely as possible from sensory impacts from the outer world. Such withdrawals of consciousness from the outer world are common to all of us in some measure, in the practices of prayer, meditation, and abstract thought.

What happens to us at these times is that, as we withdraw from the environing world, we relegate the activities of the five senses to the field of the subconscious, and seek to focus *awareness* (to the best of our ability) in the field of the superconscious—the timeless, spaceless field of the as-yet-unknown.

Awareness is the searchlight of consciousness. It is the process by means of which the individual consciousness as a whole seeks out and finds its associational affinities everywhere in the universe—raindrop, star, the time of Ptolemy, next December, the coins one pays in a purchase, the perfume of flowers, the taste of food, the meaning of a sound, the nature and significance of the macroscopic atom. Consciousness, motivated by desire and purpose, turns the searchlight of awareness on these things (and on countless others) in its attempts to identify itself with the various facts and factors that exist in areas of the universe that are objective to itself. And we know that neither the past, the present, nor the future is completely alien to the consciousness of mankind.

Such exploring activities involve concentrations of consciousness, either inward or outward. And according to the clarity with which such concentrations are sustained, a union is established between the individual consciousness thus focused and the object of its concentration. In the more common types of such concentration, *the senses* take positions that are wholly relative to the concentration effort. Awareness may use any and all of them, or none, depending upon its present need. As its present tool, it may project sight through a telescope focused on Orion, or it may concentrate hearing to catch the tune played by a distant band. And under such circumstances any or all of the other senses may be inhibited to such a degree that their perceptions do not intrude upon and disturb the present concentration of the consciousness. Awareness is the master and not the servant of the senses. It responds to their signals or not, as it chooses. It knows fields of experience that are objective to the senses; and while it cannot completely inhibit the activity of the senses, it can itself escape from their importunities.

Ordinarily, as we all know, awareness is responsive to the demands of the senses, and all of the five senses operate in areas that are objective to the individual. From sources in these outer fields the senses gather numerous stimuli, all of which affect the consciousness in some measure. But these stimuli may be broadly divided into two classes, the significant and the casual. Generally, those which are significant affect the *conscious* area of consciousness as a whole. Those that are casual may, through an arrest of awareness, affect the conscious area also; but they commonly affect only the subconscious. And to all of us it has happened that, viewing the star-filled sky on a winter night, and becoming aware of the beauty, the immensity, and the wonder of the universe, we have entirely lost sensory sight and awareness of the sky. Thought and emotion together have moved out into measureless space-time and have contemplated factors of Infinity beyond all distances and data that the senses could possibly reach.

In such types of consciousness-activity all our illusions of present time, our situation in space, and differentiations in consciousness are transcended. Awareness holds its high contact beyond the sensory field. It is neither the subconscious nor the conscious that maintains such endeavors, but the abstract human mind operating in the field of the superconscious.

There is no evidence to indicate that the finite mind of man can encompass the space-time continuum in its entirety, but there are great masses of evidence which indicate that the perceptive capacity of the human consciousness is free in far wider fields than the five senses are capable of reaching. Such excursions of awareness as we have just described are therefore "supersensory," and they occur in the field of the "superconscious." But nothing that happens to the consciousness is ever lost. Everything that is ever experienced by the human individual—whether he has been aware of it or not—affects and modifies in some measure the content and quality of his consciousness as a whole. The houses in his neighborhood are so familiar that he passes them daily without being aware of them; but his sense of sight records them in his subconscious, nevertheless, and he can recall them serially out of that storehouse at will. When one of them is repainted, or otherwise altered so that his attention is attracted to it and he becomes aware of it, that experience is recorded in both the subconscious and the conscious, and becomes subject to the recall of memory.

The data gathered in our superconscious experiences are likewise recorded in the subconscious. They are not so readily remembered as our sensory experiences are, because just as, in attempting to remember our past sensory experiences, we inhibit present sensory impressions and concentrate awareness in the subconscious (often closing our eyes or putting our hands over our ears to shut out sensory disturbances), so in recovering our past *supersensory* experience, we must likewise inhibit present sensory impressions and concentrate awareness in the subconscious.

Now all sensory impressions are made up of materials that are already familiar or arrestingly new; in either case, no item of sensory experience stands alone, but is accompanied by a host of associated data. But supersensory experiences of importance are relatively rare, for most of us, and they consequently have fewer associations than have our conscious sensory experiences; they have to be recovered from the subconscious, not with the help of associational keys—as a name may be caught by running through the alphabet for the right initial—but *in toto*, so to say; one has to recover some good measure of the *mood* of the original experience itself; and the mood is often so delicate and nebulous a matter that one must bring *both* the subconscious and the superconscious together in the present conscious field. Such an exercise of the consciousness is itself supersensory.

It may be broadly said that all activities of the individual consciousness are subjective. Their particular purpose and motivation arise within the consciousness itself, whatever objective stimulus may have led up to that motivation. For example, I do not go into trance without a purpose. Very often that purpose is suggested by someone who comes to me with a request. Such a request would be the objective stimulus, sensorily received by me (usually through the play of all of my five senses). But the process by which I induce the condition of trance is a purely personal activity on my part, which requires readjustments in my physical body, a drastic alteration of the breathing rhythm, and the inhibition of perceptions received through the five senses. In effect, by the exercise of my will, I go to sleep. And when I emerge from the trance state, I have no conscious recollection or knowledge of what has occurred, except that in "waking" I may catch a thread of connection between the two states of consciousness, as everyone does to a certain degree in those momentary dreams that crowd the doorway between sleep and full sensory awareness.

I must again remind my reader that in my own opinion consciousness is continuous, a continuum which corresponds to the space-time continuum. In both of these phases of infinitude, individual man is immersed. Thus immersed in the universal, man is a part of the whole, but only a fragment of the inseparable energy, substance, consciousness, and life that fill the universe; and his finite capacities make such contacts as they may in an environment which is always more or less limited for him individually, but which is itself everlasting and infinite, and infinitely varied in its manifestations.

The human consciousness, then, is finite in its nature. But the capacity for *abstract awareness*, which in the whole realm of mundane nature is to be found in mankind alone, is the unique faculty which allies humanity to the universal and sets the individual consciousness free in the space-time continuum. But, for the achievement and exercise of this freedom, the individual must transcend his individualism and associate himself in desire, purpose, and activity with the superindividualistic realms of consciousness that transcend his limited sensory field.

And strange as it may seem, one moves outward in *this* direction by turning inward upon oneself. In the various non-sensory activities of consciousness, there occurs a focusing of awareness in *new* objective areas of experience. And it is to be noted that the material with which awareness becomes concerned in these supersensory realms is not then available to sensory perception at all.

To remember the date of the Battle of Hastings or the name of the seventh president of the United States is not a feat of sensory perception, but of memory; and it is achieved by focusing awareness in the subjective areas of the subconscious, that storehouse of the past in which the data of our individual experience are accumulated, more or less subject to recovery.

Or if one wishes to do so, one may create a mental conception of tomorrow or of some anticipated event which is to occur in the future—one's own wedding, for example. Such a process also consists in the withdrawal of awareness from the sensory field and into the subjective concentration of attention upon areas of future time and distant space that lie completely outside the present reach of the five senses.

The competence of awareness to achieve such escapes from the field of insistent sensory perception, and to find its way in these common fields of consciousness, differs with each individual. Some people have habitually good memories or good imaginations, while the imaginations and memories of other people are relatively poor. And what these differences mean is that between the three fields of our present awareness, the stored mass of our subconscious, and the mysterious areas of the superconscious, there exist, or there do not exist (as the case may be) divisions, separations, a lack of easy interplay. Whether one's imagination or memory is "good" or "poor" depends upon the nature of the inter-relations actually operating among the three phases of his consciousness as a whole.

The supersensory experiences of clairvoyance, trance, telepathy, and so on depend upon a fundamental shift of one's awareness. The field of stimulus is itself changed. Instead of responding to sensory perceptions of the shape, color, texture, temperature, sound, taste, and odor of things in the physical world, the organism now responds to stimuli that arise in the environmental conditions which awareness discovers in the non-physical areas of the space-time continuum.

One may divert one's perceptive attention into the field of past experience and memory, or into the field of the anticipated future, or into the timeless areas of telepathic or clairvoyant awareness; and in each of these non-sensory areas, consciousness finds non-physical conditions and facts that stimulate in the perceiver's person the same types of emotional and physical reactions as are commonly stimulated by ordinary sensory perception in the outer physical field. In the practices of memory, anticipation, and telepathy alike, one finds non-physical factors that not only stir one's thought and emotion, but also stimulate in one's physical organism reactions similar to those which mark the response of the organism to perceptions in the usual sensory field.

To my own sense, this shift of sensory responsiveness from the field of physical to the field of non-physical stimulus is of primary importance, because it strikes directly at the basic dicta of the physical sciences and posits a drastic difference as existing between the *nature* of man's sensory perceptiveness and the *nature* of the world of substance.

I have frequently expressed my own belief, born of my own experience, that in a certain sense none of the parapsychological faculties are in truth "super-sensory," because in these activities the sensory end-responses operate so amply. One hears, sees, smells, tastes, and feels as in ordinary sensuous experience—only far more clearly and acutely. But in another sense—as I am indicating here—I consider that the parapsychological faculties *are* supersensory, because they operate in areas which are different from and other than the physical world, the world which science holds to be the *only* field of sensory perception.

This all leads us directly forward into the significant field of psychological imagery, and tends to establish man's fundamental conceptions of the world in which he lives, based, not in physical substance, but in human perceptual capacities that are allied to the unsubstantial nature of the space-time continuum.

When our science and mechanics have reached a measure of superlative development, as they have today, why should we hesitate to concentrate our scientific attention on the areas of human capacity out of which these achievements have been created? Thought is energy in unsubstantial form, and unsubstantial image and unsubstantial purpose are the foundations of everything that man has made—physical structures and ethical faiths alike. In concentrating all of our brilliant scientific capacities on the *substantial* products of unsubstantial idea, thought, and purpose, we have unwarrantably limited our field of perception and our understanding of human life.

The scientists have themselves driven substantiality to its sources, having analyzed it down to the basic chemical atom—a minute magnetic field. This minute magnetic field, which it is utterly impossible for the human senses to perceive in any manner as substance, is readily understood and accepted by the capacities of the mind. And this is so because the mental image of the atom is more realistic and factual and true to awareness than, for instance, any material model of it that might be set up for illustrative purposes. To consciousness, such a model is always just a crude symbol; but our mental conception of the atom partakes of the nature and mystery of the atom itself. The nature of consciousness is not substantial. First and last and always, there is the unsubstantial form behind the substantial shapes of things.

What we are seeking, in our attempts to analyze telepathy, clairvoyance, and other supersensory activities, is an understanding of the human consciousness as a whole. All of the psychic phenomena occurring in the world—so far as man is aware of them at all—occur simply as expansions or extensions of the human consciousness beyond the commonly *accepted* fields. I believe that some phases of this expansion occur to most people very commonly. Our minds are all the time full of fantasy, secondary thinking, imagination, and memory, and these are not related to the outer play of the senses in any direct way. But for the most part, this constant subsurface activity of the mind is not volitional, nor does it usually rise to the level of awareness. Usually, the flow of directly sensed images, impressions, and data takes its own way in the field of awareness, quite apart from this sub-sensory flow. By a slight act of the will, one may shift awareness from the sensed to the sub-sensory flow in one's own conciousness. And if someone offers us a penny for our thoughts, we at once become aware of the fact that we did not know of what we were really thinking.

In the well-known experiment* made by Sir Hubert Wilkins, in the Arctic, and Mr. Harold M. Sherman, sitting in his New York study, the arrangement made between them was that Wilkins was to seek solitude, and *open his subconscious.* Sherman was to ... *empty his mind of all conscious thought* and try to get the impressions that Wilkins was sending him.

This paragraph indicates in a very graphic manner the three main phases of consciousness which people are using all the time, with or without volitional purpose and direction. Wilkins was to open his *subconscious*—which can only mean that he was to suspend, as far as possible, the activities of his *conscious* mind and his sensory awareness—so that Sherman should be enabled to contact the vital areas of Wilkins' inner consciousness, without being impeded or arrested by the immediate thoughts and current sensory impressions in Wilkins' field of awareness.

---

* In Hubert Wilkins & Harold M. Sherman (1942). *Thoughts Through Space.* New York: Creative Age Press.

At the same time, Sherman was to empty his own mind of all *conscious* thought, and was to try to get the impressions that Wilkins was sending him—which can only mean that he was to transfer the awareness faculty of his consciousness into areas of time, space, and experience which were completely alien to himself and his own immediate environment. In other words, Sherman was to focus his capacities of perception in distant areas of unknown time and space—the *superconscious* field.

We have here a double plan to negate the usual varities of conscious thought and sensory awareness. On Wilkins' side there was to be a transfer of consciousness-potential into the subconscious, past, the already-experienced; and on Sherman's side there was to be a transfer of the consciousness-potential into the superconscious, the teeming void of the impersonal and the inexperienced. In both cases the activities of the conscious, the immediate affect on consciousness of sensory perception, were to be inhibited.

It is well known that Wilkins, owing to the pressure of circumstances, did not fulfill his part of the work according to plan and schedule. But Sherman sat faithfully and carried out his part of the project. And without knowing, for weeks, what measures of success he might be achieving, he continued to record his "impressions," which finally proved to contain a surprising number of correct "hits."

What renders the experiment of most importance, from our present point of view, is the fact that it goes far to prove the validity of what I am speaking of as the superconscious. For Sherman picked out of what was for him essentially a void, or a chaos, a considerable number of data concerning people, places, circumstances, and events that later proved to correspond with things that were factually happening to Wilkins himself and to his expedition, more than three thousand miles distant from Sherman's physical situation in New York.

Due to the fact that Wilkins did not carry out his part of the plan, did not "open his subconscious," the question of subconscious activity does not seem to be pertinent to the experiment or to our understanding of it. Nor was Sherman's supersensory activity telepathic. Dr. Rhine, of Duke University, has differentiated telepathy from clairvoyance in definitions which seem to me to be useful. Dr. Rhine considers telepathy to consist in the supersensory perception by one mind of what is going on in another mind, or somewhere in the field of thought. But clairvoyance he considers to be the extra-sensory perception of actual physical objects. This is as far as Dr. Rhine is ready to go in his differentiation of human capacities in the supersensory field. But if one can clairvoyantly perceive distant objects, there seems to be no reason why one should not also clairvoyantly perceive distant events and circumstances, and I personally know that these things go together.

As Sherman was not reading anybody's mind, his experiment was clairvoyant. He projected his consciousness, volitionally and purposively, into areas of the space-time continuum that were unknown to him, and he brought out of that immensity certain veridical data directly related to the purpose of his search. He was not always accurate, he was not always on time; sometimes his perception *followed* actual events, sometimes he foresaw what was still to happen in the Arctic. And as Wilkins himself had no knowledge of some of these events that still awaited him in time and space, it was not out of Wilkins' consciousness, by any sort of chance, that Sherman gathered his data. He gathered them out of areas of the space-time continuum that are not normally included in either our subconscious field of the past or the field of our conscious sensory perception of the physical world. His experiment was an exercise in "supersensory" clairvoyant perception.

An affinity exists between the individual man and the universe of so strange and subtle a nature that now, for the most part, we are able to grasp a vague impression of it only by going deep into the subconscious. But as these present years go by, the ancient content of the subconscious is being rapidly buried more and more deeply under an agglomeration of the artificial symbols of civilization. Unless psychology makes haste to fulfill its undertaken task of discovering the true psychic nature of mankind, we may have an actual split in the human race, with a new racial type following a developmental path of freedom for the mind, in supersensory fields, while the rest of mankind remains to perfect the physical field of substance and the senses.

In fact there are evidences which indicate that such a division is at the very root of the present world-conflict. But when this war is ended and mankind is again very poor, according to its own standards of poverty and wealth (having wasted its physical substance in a general destruction), we may find that through pain and suffering and death we have come to a clearer realization of humanity's super-physical sources in the past and humanity's super-physical destiny in the future. If this turns out to be so in any immediate sense, the foundations of a finer future will already have been laid—in which case we shall have been led forward toward a wider comprehension of the space-time continuum and the unity and continuity of the consciousness continuum also. And these objective factors, which transcend our dependence on the five senses, as they are now conceived, may very well prove to be the beginning of a new freedom in the vast fields of consciousness, for humanity as a whole.

Among all our psychological faculties, awareness is the capacity for cognizance. As such it transcends the limitations which time and space impose upon the senses, and is able to gather experience in areas of being which the senses can never reach. Its nature is to poise, like a hunting hawk, ready to be sent abroad in any direction, to impale the attractive fact, idea, or event, and to bring back to consciousness the trophy of its flight. It can move in any and all of the three dimensions of consciousness represented by memory, the senses, and imagination; and when controlled by the will, its efficiency can become a creative force in the individual life.

If, briefly, we shut out all sensory intrusions, and focus awareness upon our inner selves, we shall acquire a sense of the dark and featureless vitality that moves in our bodies. And if, then, we ask ourselves, "What do I most want in this world and this life?" we shall experience the flight of the hawk—sensations created by awareness moving to find the answer. This movement may be in either of two directions, but not in the third. If we have thought constructively of this idea before, awareness may move into memory to find the answer; but if the question is not repetitive, awareness will make its flight toward the open spaces of inspiration. It may not bring back the answer, for the question is deep and subtle; but if we continue to sustain our resistance to sensory intrusions, and keep perception centered on the hawk, we shall perceive at least the direction in which inspiration lies, and undoubtedly the first creative stirrings of response.

Awareness and perception are brothers. Either one may wake the other to a quest. But they are both sound sleepers—not because they want to be, but because we hood and jess them—too restrictively, fail to make them fly, and so they lose their ranging natures. We need to fly them both more freely—especially in this dawn of a new day which promises humanity at large a wider field of psychological freedom than mankind has ever known before …

II
Sleep and Dreams

IT IS NATURAL that in relation to any event as common and recurrent as sleep the question "Why?" should often have been asked. But nobody seems to know very precisely why a human being goes to sleep, or what happens to him when he does so. Many theories have been suggested by way of answer to the question. Ancient Eastern philosophies teach that in sleep the soul leaves the body and goes to its own place to learn, to teach, or to heal. The more modern theories of neurology, chemistry, and biology suggest various causes—such as a reduction of the efficiency of the neurons in transmitting nerve impulses, owing to fatigue; chemical changes in the composition of the blood stream; and the cyclic rhythms of activity and quiescence which occur in the life-processes of all natural forms.

But regardless of whatever deep discoveries the sciences may make in relation to sleep, we all know that we go to sleep because we are "tired" in body, mind, and interest. This tiredness is often very largely a matter of boredom; but boredom, too, signifies that we have had a surfeit of whatever has been occupying our attention, and we often go to sleep simply to escape, for the present, from a world which is no longer either imperatively demanding or sufficiently interesting.

When we go to sleep, there occurs in our consciousness a fundamental dissociation of faculties. The faculty that I am speaking of as awareness in this book—the capacity to centralize interest and attention responsively or at will—ceases to operate. Thus shorn of awareness, we seem to come very close to the condition of death, for we have no means of knowing what happens to us during these silent hours of relaxation and inactivity. As we look at the sleeper, all the signs of life but one are absent from his appearance—he breathes. The breath is our assurance of life; and since by the breath we know that he is not dead, but sleeps, we know also that he is inwardly experiencing, even though unconsciously, the re-creation of the forces of his life.

Sleep is thus allied to the recuperation of our vital energies. And though it is so common, so "natural," that we sink into it without thought or question, it is difficult for us to understand how all of our waking faculties can disappear into the depths of unconsciousness, so that we are completely cut off from all knowledge of the world, and yet nothing happens to us, so far as we ourselves then know.

But there is one thread that ties our sleeping state to awareness. It is the thread of dreams; and by means of this thread, mankind has been enabled to perceive, however dimly, that at least one of the three phases into which we have divided consciousness as a whole continues to function. This is the subconscious phase. And the apparently wild, irrational, and bizarre quality of many of our dreams is a clue to the nature of the subconscious, for as the subconscious is revealed to us in dreams we usually perceive it as a world that is not only unfamiliar, but often utterly unknown.

Following is a report by Havelock Ellis which indicates the general oddness of many of our dreams:

> A lady dreamed that an acquaintance wished to send a small sum of money to a person in Ireland. She rashly offered to take it over to Ireland. On arriving home she began to repent of her promise, as the weather was extremely wild and cold. She proceeded, however, to make preparations for dressing warmly, and went to consult an Irish friend, who said she would have to be floated over to Ireland tightly jammed in a crab basket. On returning home she fully discussed the matter with her husband, who thought it would be folly to undertake such a journey, and she finally relinquished it, with great relief.*

This dream gives very clear indications of the sub-rational level at which the mind operates in sleep. Apparently, the immediate modern world may or may not be included in the subconscious levels that appear in our dreams. Nevertheless, a sequential *rationale* does seem to operate in the subconscious; and though the dream quoted above happened at a level of consciousness which apparently contained no knowledge of modern postal systems and transportation facilities, it runs a logical course from beginning to end—at its own level.

What causes us to dream?

Under the old scientific dictum which held that nothing enters into the mind except by way of the five senses, it has come to be believed that any dream sufficiently intense to affect awareness must have a sensory stimulus. And sensory stimuli do affect the activities occurring in the physical body during sleep. We have all been waked by *feeling* cold or by *hearing* some noise in the outer world. And it has been reliably found by test that the rattle of a window sash, the ticking of a clock, or an indirect light will have a more or less disturbing effect upon a sleeper's rest.

It is well known, therefore, that the senses are awake and operating during our sleep. In fact it is supposed that the five senses never wholly aban-

---

* In Havelock Ellis (1911). *The World of Dreams*. New York: Houghton Mifflin.

don their work of testing the immediate environment of the organism to which they belong. By means of these ever-watchful sentinels, the individual consciousness is always united to the outer world, and never isolated from it—and this in spite of the fact that in sleep we close our eyes and relax all the tensions of body, emotions, and mind, surrendering awareness.

So sensory stimuli affect the subconscious in sleep, stirring there irrational images that are compounded of emotional and mental qualities, which are the stuff of past experiences consciously or subconsciously lived through by the sleeper, or inherited by him from the racial past.

In order to get a working conception of the subconscious we may isolate it, imaginatively, by thinking of it as the storehouse of all our past experiences, forever open to effect from the universe beyond itself, in which a creative life-process is constantly in operation. This creative life-process is at once the development of the inner nature of the individual, and the development of his environment also, in the measure in which he effectively acts in that environment.

There are no records to indicate how or when this intimate relationship between the outer world and individual forms of human life began. All that we know of the ancient past of mankind leads us to believe that life has developed in a continuously evolving process, through a long procession of living forms that have expressed the energies of life, and that this evolutionary process has developed upward through a progressive complexity of physical parts, a multiplicity of action capacities, and an increase of faculties for wider relationships. It is also held that in its early development the human embryo passes through several stages of sub-human form—fish, reptile, bird—and thus symbolically "re-experiences" or recapitulates the whole evolutionary past through which life has forged its slow but steady way up to our present human level.

So we suppose that deep in the subconscious of each human being there resides an accumulated basic sum of consciousness-potential which summarizes the whole evolutionary history of mankind, and which is now prepared to receive and express the present evolutionary phases of human development, as the individual experiences the current world—always, of course, according to the particular quality and nature of his capacities. But here, too, it must be remembered, much of our current experience is worldwide and racial in its nature.

From such basic beginnings each human individual proceeds, from birth, to develop his current relationships and gather experience; and his perception and his interpretation of each event of his life, no matter how important or how trivial it may seem, may alter the basic quality of his nature and modify the sum of his subconscious content.

It is this mass of past experience, racial and personal, that constitutes the phase of consciousness into which we sink in sleep. It is this mass also that produces dreams, and that secondary flow of fantasy, vagrant imagination, and strange ideation which, like a second mind within us, constantly operates behind the primary play of our waking thought and awareness. This "mind" of the subconscious is never still. Unlike awareness and the conscious mind, the subconscious never sleeps. It has developed out of that seed which was also the beginning of the individual physical form; and the physical form and the subconscious are consequently so closely allied as to be inseparable. And just as, in life, a man's physical organism continues to function without ceasing, so its twin, the subconscious, functions without ceasing also.

It is out of this inseparable relation between the physical body and the subconscious that our dreams arise. In sleep, the messages that are brought from the outer world by the five senses affect the subconscious, and the subconscious, thus affected, reacts. But it reacts at its own level of sensitivity and interpretation; and this level lies below the level of the rational mind, so our dreams are usually unrealistic, incoherent, or bizarre.

Yet when one's sleep is normal, this whole process is completely natural. Fundamentally, there is nothing strange about it. All sensory perception stirs emotional response within the organism; in every case of sensory perception the consciousness reacts, clothing the perception with images; in sleep, the subconscious clothes the perception in images that are not rationalized. In each case, these images are related to some particular phase of the whole past of the individual, inherited and personal, and the nature of a dream depends upon the particular depth at which a present emotional drive affects the subconscious content.

Thus, in the dream which has been cited, we can only suppose that the dreamer's subconscious was stimulated at a level that was more ancient than modern. Her moral sense operated, for though she didn't like the prospect of being floated over to Ireland tightly jammed in a crab basket, in the wild cold weather, she went ahead and prepared for the journey as she had promised. Yet again, at her husband's advice she abandoned the whole scheme, and the problem, in both its moral and practical aspects, evaporated into its own inconsequence. We may assume that in this solution of the problem the dreamer had already begun to waken; and she presently emerged into full wakefulness and became aware in the conscious present, from which point she no doubt looked back upon the dream as strange and outlandish. If, however, as science believes, our subconscious content extends infinitely backward into the past, there is no reason for us to be surprised—though we often are—by the appearance in our dreams of places, persons, conditions, and events of which we have had no conscious experience.

Both in sleeping and waking, different individuals exhibit various degrees of psychic perception and appreciation. The secret of one type of such facility seems to lie in consanguinity. It is not without basis that the breeding of blood-strains has long been a major occupation of the human mind.

But the sensitivities which consanguinity may give to consciousness are not exclusive. They may be practically duplicated in the relation established between married people, and between friends whose relationship is intimate, sincere, and deep. In all such cases there occurs a psychic identification of each consciousness with the other, and a new synthesis of consciousness is thus created—a synthesis in which the ingredient parts are fused and transcend themselves into a *new* consciousness-capacity that transcends all the apparent qualities and values of its components.

Such mutual identifications of diverse personalities, through the blood and through the development of a close emotional sympathy, are the most easily apprehended foundations of a psychic interplay which extends into wide areas of significance. But supersensory activities are not dependent on consanguinity or emotional affinity. There are on record, from both ancient and recent times, many dreams of a type that differs radically from our usual vague and fanciful ones and which, instead of being concerned with the subconscious past, participate in the immediate present, and include awareness of events occurring in the present world, but beyond the independent reach of the senses.

The following telepathic experience, which originated in the dream state, was reported by F. W. H. Myers many years ago, and is an interesting case in point:[*]

> About a year ago there died in a neighboring village a brewer called Wünscher, with whom I stood in friendly relations. His death ensued after a short illness, and as I seldom had an opportunity of visiting him, I knew nothing of his illness nor of his death. On the day of his death I went to bed at nine o'clock, tired with the labors which my calling as a farmer demands of me. Here I must observe that my diet is of a frugal kind; beer and wine are rare things in my house, and water, as usual, had been my drink that night. Being of a very healthy constitution, I fell asleep as soon as I lay down. In my dream I heard the deceased call out with a loud voice, "Boy, make haste and give me my boots." This awoke me, and I

[*] In F. W. H. Myers (1899–1900). "A defense of phantasms of the dead." *Proceedings of the Society for Psychical Research, 6,* 314–357.

noticed that, for the sake of our child, my wife had left the light
burning. I pondered with pleasure over my dream, thinking
in my mind how Wünscher, who was a good-natured, humor-
ous man, would laugh when I told him of this dream. Still
thinking of it, I hear Wüncher's voice scolding outside, just
under my window. I sit up in my bed at once and listen, but
cannot understand his words. What can the brewer want? I
thought, and I know for certain that I was much vexed with
him, that he should make a disturbance in the night, as I felt
convinced that his affairs might surely have waited till the
morrow. Suddenly he comes into the room from behind the
linen press, steps with long strides past the bed of my wife
and the child's bed; wildly gesticulating with his arms all the
time, as his habit was, he called out, "What do you say to this,
Herr Oberamptmann? This afternoon at five o'clock I have
died." Startled by this information, I exclaim, "Oh, that is
not true!" He replied: "Truly, as I tell you; and, what do you
think? They want to bury me already on Tuesday afternoon at
two o'clock," accenting his assertions all the while by his ges-
ticulations. During this long speech of my visitor I examined
myself as to whether I was really awake and not dreaming.

I asked myself: Is this a hallucination? Is my mind in
full possession of its faculties? Yes, there is the light, there
the jug, this is the mirror, and this the brewer; and I came
to the conclusion: I am awake. Then the thought occurred
to me, What will my wife think if she awakes and sees the
brewer in our bedroom? In this fear of her waking up I turn
round to my wife, and to my great relief I see from her face,
which is turned toward me, that she is still asleep; but she
looks very pale. I say to the brewer, "Herr Wünscher, we will
speak softly, so that my wife may not wake up, it would be
very disagreeable to her to find you here." To which Wünscher answered in a lower and calmer tone: "Don't be afraid,
I will do no harm to your wife." Things do happen indeed
for which we find no explanation—I thought to myself,
and said to Wünscher: "If this be true, that you have died,
I am sincerely sorry for it; I will look after your children."
Wünscher stepped toward me, stretched out his arms and
moved his lips as though he would embrace me; therefore
I said in a threatening tone, and looking steadfastly at him
with a frowning brow: "Don't come so near, it is disagreeable to me," and lifted my right arm to ward him off, but
before my arm reached him the apparition had vanished. My

first look was to my wife to see if she were still asleep. She was. I got up and looked at my watch, it was seven minutes past twelve. My wife woke up and asked me: "To whom did you speak so loud just now?" "Have you understood anything?" I said. "No," she answered, and went to sleep again.

I report this experience to the Society for Psychical Research, in the belief that it may serve as a new proof for the real existence of telepathy. I must further remark that the brewer had died that afternoon at five o'clock, and was buried on the following Tuesday at two. With great respect.

Karl Dignowity
(Landed Proprietor)

In this case there does not seem to have been any very close relationship between Dignowity and Wünscher. The former says simply that he "stood in friendly relations" with the brewer. It would be impossible for us to determine just why or how this particular experience occurred. It is, however, my personal opinion that supersensory sensitivity is much more common with people than we generally suppose, and that many of our dreams and "intuitions" are really the germs of true supersensory experience.

Most dreaming is evidently a subconscious process, but there are dreams which occur in the super-sensory field, clairvoyant and telepathic dreams— sleeping states in which awareness goes out from its place of individualistic centralization and makes contact with distant minds, forms, circumstances, and events, knowledge of which it brings back to deliver before consciousness itself awakes. Very often these images are difficult to understand, because they are precise and definite in content, not symbolic. They are not open to interpretation, therefore, but constitute a significant message in themselves, the relation of which to the rest of life and action is not clear. But eventually their values—their meaning and reality—are revealed through subsequent association with people and conditions. Understanding eventuates as they fit into the pattern of life to which they belong.

In the waking practice of telepathy and clairvoyance one usually has a fairly specific objective goal for the focus of concentration, and it is not difficult to conceive of lines of magnetic force (or whatever one may wish to call the phenomenon) being established between two phases of consciousness, so that a more or less direct relation and rapport are set up between them. In pursuing similar types of super-sensory activity in the sleeping state, however, one has to deposit one's intention with the subconscious, and trust it to carry out the project.

Dreams in the sleeping state are supposed to be motivated in the subconscious in response to sensory stimuli. But I believe we may add to these *the stimuli of purposive intentions in the conscious mind*. Such intentions, deposited with the subconscious, have frequently brought me dreams which were ample, if not complete, fulfillments of the experience which I sought. One of the most interesting aspects of such experiences is the fact that what I sought was usually somebody else's concern, quite impersonal to me, so that the dream material eventually depended for all its values upon the acceptance and understanding of another person. Under such circumstances I have found spread before awareness, on waking, the odd and intimate names of people, places, and things, dissociated dates, cryptic phrases and catchwords—things I had never heard of before, things which meant absolutely nothing to me. But in reporting these to the person on whose behalf I had sought them, they proved to be coherent and significant to that other consciousness.

It may be somewhat confusing to amplify thus the field of dreams by including within it the purposive intentions of the conscious mind as well as clairvoyance and telepathy. But in a later chapter I shall indicate how my own work in waking telepathy and clairvoyance begins with a breath that descends to the region of the solar plexus, which I consider to be the seat of the subconscious in a certain sense; and I have discovered in my own practice that when I commit telepathic or clairvoyant work to the subconscious, to be executed while I sleep, such commitments are accompanied at the physical level by a solar plexus breath.

This passage of the breath to the solar plexus area, and of the conscious to the subconscious, are but a step in a process in which further efforts, both physical and psychic, proceed to develop into superconscious activity. I have no doubt that this process develops in sleep as in our waking states—in consequence of which we have telepathic and clairvoyant dreams, volitionally and non-sensorily induced.

What I have gathered for myself out of these and other experiences is the conviction that we commonly conceive the senses as far more physical in their nature than they really are. The physical aspects of eye and ear undoubtedly have their deep and subtle psychic counterparts, sensitive and capable of reacting to mysterious stimuli which are truly "sensory," though not in the commonly understood meaning of that word. One may be waked out of a sound sleep by the soundless need of a distant consciousness, and one may bring out of sleep, into waking awareness, factual data concerning distant and unknown people, places, and events. To my own sense, what we require for understanding such occurrences is primarily a new conception of the sensory capacities. But for the present we have no adequate clues to such an extension, though the whole perceptive process is rapidly increasing the evidences of these more subtle activities.

As the Dignowity experience indicates, definite auditory sensation may take place in sleep as well as in our receptive waking states. And I am myself convinced that the stimulus of someone's need for speech with me may produce subjective effects similar to those which follow the conscious reception of verbal speech. We believe that memory is the function of recalling, reproducing, identifying, and coordinating what has already been learned or experienced. On the other hand, telepathy may be our hitherto unsuspected ability to absorb stimulus and significance from both our instinctive inheritance and our sympathetic environment—from the whole vast storehouse of the universal past, present, and future.

I am inclined to give sincere credence to this thought, for various reasons: when I endeavor to work clairvoyantly by "rules," or to "guess" a certain number of symbols, I have no inner awareness of any stimulus at work. But if the idea comes to me that the symbols or formulae are contained within someone else's mind, it adds vigor to the undertaking. No experiment, in which I know the *nature of the experiment* in advance, can ever produce the feeling of alertness and anticipation that a significant message is coming through from the unknown. *That* experience is best described as a positive *knowing*.

Moreover, as I have indicated above, I have frequently directed myself before sleeping to seek certain results from the dream material, which I would remember in my waking state. I have directed the self, on the point of going to sleep, to go forth in certain directions and find answers to certain questions, or the solution of specific problems that were *not my own*, which I should clearly retain and recollect on waking. In other words, I have simply applied the processes of the learned response to the subconscious.

No one who has nursed a beloved sick child, and had to wake to its needs without the aid of sensory warnings, can doubt the ever-present watchfulness of the inner mind. And who, observing the sleeping infant rouse when feeding time arrives, can doubt that the inner mind is ever watchful? Indeed, I have found that fixed habit patterns can be overcome as soon as we make known to the subconscious the change which we desire. I believe, therefore, that the subconscious is our most alert, loyal, and willing servant, able and ready to obey and cooperate in both our sleeping and waking activities. It becomes unwieldy and a master only when we do not trouble to understand and train it.

I have sometimes been asked if my supersensory experiences are not hallucinations. To this I can only answer that, since they bring to consciousness their own responses, experiences, and emotional significances, as the sensory events of my life do, I cannot deny their reality for the sake of a merely negative terminology that does not make itself clear to me. Since I believe that sleep is a state of suspension, to rest the motor activities of the body, it is easy for me to understand that sleep is also the condition in which the mind lives out in undisturbed fantasy and symbol those aspects of our inner lives that we hide away because of limitation, lack of courage, or fears imposed by man's law. Man's law, unfortunately, is not of the universal order, and it is to the universal order that we are constantly being called for accounting. The universal order is not confined to the sensory field, and to train the consciousness to perceive and be aware in the super-sensory field seems to me to be a normal and progressive activity in human living.

Imagination deals with distances of time and space, with great areas beyond time and space, with the inexperienced and the supersensory, and it is therefore potentially creative in the supersensory field. But the experiences of imaginative states enter into and alter the subconscious content, and if persistently practiced, they may so color the subconscious with non-factual data that delusion results. It would seem to me, however, that only in lives that are so insensitive, so barren, and so inexpressive as to be unable to find sufficient experience in the present, or in lives bound by conditions that deny any adequate expression to innate impulses, that imagination could thus become the dominant experience-material entering into the consciousness.

On the other hand, imagination may be made a creative factor, in connection with sleep, provided it is based at once in the realities of normal living and in our legitimate aspirations. The quality of the subconscious is cumulative and, to some extent at least, its content may be constructively designed as we go on living. I have myself cultivated the habit of controlling my subconscious, and through the years I have progressively developed a unity among the several levels of my own consciousness. This seems to have developed as a facility in consciousness itself—a unitary instead of a divided power. Sleep, dreams, sensory perception, telepathy, and trance have become a set of instrumentalities or techniques which I use, like a rack of tools, to accomplish my work in the most efficient way.

This statement would be inadequate, however, if I failed to emphasize the fact that such practice rests squarely on the unselfish legitimacy of one's purposes. There are vast moral and psychological differences between what the ancients termed black and white magic, and there is nothing more destructive of life, both for the individual and for the factors of his environment, than a high efficiency that is used for selfish, exclusive, restrictive, and repressive purposes. All expressions of human life are in fact magical, if we look at them closely enough to see it. The civilized world which mankind has created out of natural substances is the most magical thing that has ever come into existence. And the individual life of each one of us is a factor in that whole magical work, which we can darken through our ignorance and egotism or brighten by the honest exercise of service in behalf of the freedom of life in all its aspects. With every ignorant or careless negation we restrict ourselves as well as others; with every release of life into fuller freedom we are ourselves set free.

I never go to sleep without taking thought for tomorrow. Gauging the relative importances of various things that I have to do, I place the most important, *as the most important*, in my subconscious, with other importances following after. And the consequence is that, day by day, I live a life which is *my* life. Since I thus have my own work to do, I am not subject to many chance incursions from the outer world, and I have very little time for those mischiefs which Satan finds for idle hands and idle minds to do.

This preview of tomorrow affects the superconscious as well as the subconscious; and it is because this is so that the consciousness as a whole is strengthened in unity. If a necessary piece of work requires the presence of a friend or a business acquaintance at my office at eleven o'clock tomorrow morning, I send word to that person telepathically, and usually he is present as expected, or else I hear from him.

But in all of this there must be a fundamental purity of selflessness. I do not send for the man because *I* want him to come, but because a constructive situation requires his presence for its further development. And though it is I who send for him and who assume the responsibility for the event, I do not mind doing this, since I never take such action except in terms of conscious good faith and unselfish good will.

I should never use these cultivated capacities to command any person against his will; and since I have not surrendered to the forces of ignorance or mere curiosity, I believe that my continued capacity to operate in this way depends upon the purity of my motives. In such activity, no illusions must be permitted and no mistakes must be made.

In living habitually in this way one comes to know and understand one's own impulsions and purposes, and the effects of environmental factors in one's life. One develops a supersensory point of view, from which one becomes *consciously* critical of both sensory effect and the nature of one's own response; and eventually, the effect of all this is the depersonalization of one's life, the transcendence of one's egotism, and the performance of one's duties with a larger joy than self-centeredness can ever know.

III
Hypnosis and Suggestion

AS IN SLEEP and in anesthesia, there are several different levels or depths at which it is possible for consciousness to be active under hypnosis also. The recuperative values which accrue to us during sleep are of primary importance to our lives; those people who have had any kind of "psychic" experience under anesthesia know that that experience consisted of an unforgettable perceptive glimpse of a world—a condition of consciousness—that was vastly different from the conditions of our ordinary living at the levels of sensory perception. Likewise in hypnotic states, our lives not only may be, but actually are, affected by means that are far removed from the levels of sensory perception.

In the nineteenth century—the early days of the Victorian era—an intense rivalry was fought out between hypnosis and ether as anesthetic agents. But they have now become pretty clearly separated into the fields of their respective best usefulness, the more materialistic ether having become the agent for the physical induction of temporary dissociation, and hypnotic suggestion having become a technique of treatment for the correction of dissociations of abnormal psychological types.

Suggestion is not only a method of treatment for psychological abnormalities, however, but is at once the cause as well as the cure of them. It is the source of our highest aspirations and our best achievements; it is a seed of all the bright and dark activities of human beings in this world. We find our way through life by following suggestions that are constantly being made to consciousness, either by ourselves or by people and events in the outer world. Suggestion is the key to all education and the root of value in all experience.

In a certain sense, all suggestion is hypnotic, and all of our activities are the results of suggestion. For hypnosis, it is not necessary to engage the services of a trained and expert hypnotist, except for some unusual kind of special treatment, for we are all constantly hypnotizing ourselves and each other. When one gets out of bed in the morning, feeling inadequately rested from the drain of a season of hard work, one's body may cry out for more rest, and one may wish intensely to go back to bed. These are natural expressions of the need of the organism. But consciousness knows that the job to be done is waiting, and one transcends the weariness of his body by some such hypnotic phrase as "I *must* go to work," and in consciousness the idea of bodily weariness is displaced by a sense—and probably a picture—of the work that awaits him. So he goes to his place of business, whatever that may be, and carries on with the job; and the exhaustion that he felt so keenly an hour or two ago fades from his consciousness completely—is forgotten. He has hypnotized himself into doing another day's work.

I have a friend who is thoroughly convinced that the only right mood in which to keep a social engagement—dinner party, cards, or the theatre—is one of rebellion, resentment, and distaste. Having hypnotized himself into such a mood, he keeps his appointment, quite sure at heart of having a pleasant evening; for having prepared himself to endure the worst in boredom and ennui, he has found, without exception, that no party is ever as bad as that, and he always has a better time than anticipated.

Conversely, many young people suffer their worst disillusionments through having hypnotized themselves into expecting too much from the dance or the week-end—often more than was mortally possible. We actually make most of our own successes and distresses by the manner in which we anticipate and prepare our approach to the various events of our lives. We have to learn, by observing our own acceptances and rejections of experience, what we really do want out of life and the world. And then it is only by seeing ourselves in the mirror of the world's response to our advances that we become aware of both sides of the picture of ourselves. As we proceed in this salutary training of consciousness we do learn to know ourselves, and also, the faults and values of our own hypnotic powers: the glamour and illusion of our ignorance gradually fade out, and the motivations of our lives come to rest more and more firmly on reality. But this "reality" is always a strictly private and personal creation—the result of the experience of the individual consciousness in the business of living, and the result of his interpretations of that experience.

Many of us are far too credulous before the world's harsh treatment of our early illusions; we accept its reactions to our ambitions and our hopes as more important and more realistic than we are. If we are sensitive, we are apt to sink into a relative negativity under the treatment we receive from the sophisticated, and often hesitate to give expression to the intuitions and aspirations that move in us. We thus become hypnotized into shyness, which is a form of fear—that basest of advisers—and we live a kind of life of the herd through the years, never becoming our individual selves in an adequate measure, and dying at last, having scarcely felt or intimated the brilliance and beauty that lie hidden in the diamond depths of our individual souls.

Each one of us, consciously or unconsciously, creates and nourishes the quality of his own subconscious. The subconscious is the storehouse of our individualism, in which all that happens to us becomes a part of what we are. But always, our interpretation of a particular experience, and our reaction to it, are psychologically more important than the experience itself. If, looking outward in certain directions, we find ourselves afraid of what we may encounter there, we are usually suffering some hypnotic illusions. But such conditions can be offset by self-hypnosis of a more constructive type, and if we will, we can go out courageously, gaily, or in a spirit of acceptance to meet the experience toward which we are inwardly motivated.

There are few of us who have not had the privilege, at some time, of meeting with great *savoir faire* some mean or potentially destructive situation which has been forced upon us. And who has not had the experience of responding to tragedy or danger with greater dignity, calmness, and courage than he knew he possessed? When the demand for divinity becomes imperative, the native divinity that is in us emerges. In our hours of deepest need we call upon it, consciously or unconsciously, and are saved by it. This divinity is not objective to us. We are immersed in it and infused with it. But in order to permit it to operate, we have to clear the petty and personal impediments of our lives from the channels of consciousness itself and approach to unity with the divine Universal.

This is a fact in nature; and while it is "religious" in the sense that it is concerned with the mystery of the divine Unity of Life, it exists beyond all creeds and dogmas. I am reminded of the adventure of Captain E. V. Rickenbacker who, with other Army men, was lost on the empty waters of the South Pacific for twenty-three days, in a tiny rubber raft. These men suffered everything from thirst, hunger, and exposure; but when they were finally rescued, Captain Rickenbacker is reported to have said, "I am not formally a religious man, but I can truthfully say that I never doubted for one moment we'd be saved." This is one instance of the inner faith which has become a common experience of men in the current war, one instance of many in which consciousness has become aware of its own depths. As we penetrate beyond the surfaces of sensory experience and habit, we come into the areas of natural telepathy; and when we are most simply ourselves—most closely face to face with life—we find our basic assurances and *know* what we know.

Young and old, we are all continually met with negation. When we ask for positive action we are told "It can't be done," or "I can't do that," and far too frequently we accept the negation. This is due to the peculiar way in which we are trained from birth. Listen to the average mother correct her child: "No, dear, you can't do that." "Why not?" "Because Mother says you can't." "But why, Mother?" Then it comes, inevitably: "Do you want to be punished? Do you want me to tell Daddy you've been a naughty boy?" This is suggestive education of the worst kind. Meanwhile the child fails to learn why he should not run on the grass, put his hand in the fire, or do the countless other things he is inwardly moved to do. He grows up not only confused and conditioned to negation, but with a completely distorted sense of values. Modern education has done something to correct this evil, but it forgets that the child is a little animal and must be taught self-discipline as well as facts. He is not yet an integrated individual, and to give him too much freedom of expression, without adequate guidance, is to license him to act without responsibility. But responsibility is inherent in the very nature of relationships, and it cannot be ignored without lessening the values of life. I assert again that we are outward and visible forms of omnipotence, and to deny or disregard this universalistic power is to disregard one's very self.

Experimenting in experience is the process of individuation and of universalization. When I speak in this book of transcending our individualism, I am really referring to the full and conscious individualizing of ourselves. These two processes are inseparably complementary. We can develop our individualism only by contacts with states of being that are objective to the sum of what we are at the present moment. In every extension of ourselves into those objective fields, we take in something of their quality, and our own quality is thus modified through amplification. Every true expression of ourselves is a step toward the fuller universalization of our consciousness. When we no longer allow ourselves to be dominated and inhibited by the herd-attitudes, but spend our lives in the free expression of our very selves, we shall find that selfishness is a barrier that restricts the freedom of life, while true freedom is compounded of service and joy.

One of the soundest criticisms of our modern civilized scheme of things is the mounting number of cases of insanity and nervous and mental disorders that crowd our asylums and the offices of the psychiatrists. The too restrictive confining of natural human impulses; the confusing and inhibiting dictatorship of public opinion; the harnessing of sensitive and intelligent individuals to routine work; the limiting of human freedom through financial stringency—these common conditions of civilized life (and I am not writing here of war conditions, but of the usual "peacetime" state of things) are creating a progressive strain and tension in human life itself. We are building up tremendous collective efficiencies at the expense of individual living. Life, liberty, and the pursuit of happiness are fundamentally for the human being only; and it is the present problem of the individual to find the means for his self-expression—which most of us succeed in doing in a saving, though limited, measure.

Most human lives in the world are relatively dull because, confined as we are to the necessities of earning a living in a collective and economic world, our consciousness is dominated by perception at the sensory level, and the whole mass of our developing subconscious—the actual potential quality of our individuality—is controlled by the collective policy.

For the individual, the only escape from this mass-dominance lies in his conscious practice of self-hypnotism. But such an undertaking must be motivated by impulses arising within the individual himself, and they must be creative, unselfish, and universalistic in purpose; otherwise, he will find himself only more deeply imbedded in the pressures of the herd-mind.

In past years I used sometimes to stare at myself with a kind of objective curiosity, wondering if I were constituted differently from the rest of mankind. I knew I possessed supersensory capacities, and these seemed to be very rare phenomena in the world. But I could find no marks of abnormality in myself; I caught no clues anywhere in my social relations to indicate that I was "queer" or strange. Following a self-examination, and accepting all the indications that showed my life to be normal, I questioned why more people were not also developing and expressing themselves in the field of super-sensory experience. And I finally came to the conclusion that most people are afraid—afraid of both the subconscious and the superconscious areas of their innate being. For most of us there is a narrow band of consciousness-experience, at the sensory level, which constitutes the general field of our perception and our knowledge. And as this narrow area deals mainly with our civilized, and not our natural relationships, the subconscious content of most "civilized" men and women is rapidly becoming denatured—not to say dehumanized.

Naturally, it is not my intention to advise any man who is intent on catching the 5:15 train instead of looking at the sunset, or any woman who has to hurry home from the afternoon bridge game instead of noticing the violet shadows that the trees cast on the snow in the winter dusk, to abandon these "practical" activities and attempt to become "psychic." The only purpose I have in these pages consists in making clear statements of human existence as I see it—the basis for this point of view being my own knowledge, won through experience, of the fact that human life is potentially far richer than we commonly encourage it to be in practice. This reality is now beginning to be apprehended by many people, in a vague way, and it seems to me pertinent to juxtapose, at this time, certain facts and factors of my own experience and the emerging scientific knowledge in a pattern which, though small, may prove to be both rational and cogent.

No one who understands the operation of super-sensory activities would lightly recommend the undertaking of this type of endeavor. In the first place, and for most people, it constitutes a radical departure in living—an immediate and developing readjustment of all of one's points of view; the displacement of countless uncertainties with sure knowledge; a drastic alteration in the content of the subconscious; and a fresh new batch of realizations concerning nearly everything with which one comes in contact.

It will be obvious that, in the face of such readjustments as these, one must be ready to make countless surrenders in the ways and habits of his life. The pattern is a pattern of uniqueness. In working it out, one gradually emerges from the depths of participation in the collective consciousness and becomes more and more individualized. But for the person who, through purity of purpose, actually develops a high measure of individualization, the period of individual self-consciousness is relatively brief. One naturally gazes at oneself in amazement for a while. But the very experience which differentiates him as an individual on the one hand, on the other hand universalizes his consciousness at the same time. And even while he realizes his employment of new mechanisms, he also appreciates the breadth and importance of his expanding relationships beyond mere personality.

I believe that many people close their minds to psychic experience because they are afraid of their own capacities; others have the fear that in becoming universalistic they will become somehow dehumanized; while some, no doubt, hesitate to accept the added responsibility which inevitably accompanies every expansion of consciousness. But to be controlled by such fears and hesitancies is to indulge a lack of faith in human nature; it is to imagine oneself to be like the Normandy poplar, whose skyward reach is often too heavy for its roots.

Actually, however, this is not a practical danger —unless one is already psychologically so unstable as to be stimulated by illusional rather than realistic motives. For in the actual work of psychic development, self-discipline is the first regimen, and self-purification is the first law. There is of course nothing strange or mysterious about these facts, for in any psychical undertaking one necessarily moves away from obvious objective perception and turns his awareness to the perception of the subtle; and since the nuances of his own psychic activity constitute his most immediate subtle field, this becomes the natural area for the practice and the establishment of his psychic controls.

The first objective of the control of the subtle consists in the penetration by awareness of one's habitual sensory perceptions—the going through and beyond the first obvious *impressions* of things and the discerning of the contents of the second, third, and further depths in the perceptual field. Do you see the individual blossoms in a mass of garden bloom? The patches of blue and yellow in a tree's greenness? Have you differentiated the little planes of amethyst, blue, white, and green light that constitute the peacock coloring of a wave? In a landscape that you are looking at, do you see beyond the buildings and the trees that hide the rest from your eyes—the pasture where the cows are grazing, the path the brook follows as it runs down to the pond, how many willows lean along its borders, whether there are mushrooms in the meadow today? Can you see the whole wide spread of countryside in detail, and in different lights—at different times of day and on different kinds of days, winter, summer, midnight, dawn? Can you feel the dew in the grass when there is no dew, and hear the orioles call when all orioles are far away, and feel the lovely eeriness of moonlight on a hayfield, and smell the sweetness of the mown hay, while riding on a Fifth Avenue bus or taking your train at the Grand Central Terminal?

Such simple practices are among the early stages of one's control of one's senses and other perceptive capacities. Someone may ask, "But is it valuable to hear the oriole call when he is not there, or to feel the dew in the grass when there is no dew?" But I ask, "Is it not?" The loveliness that I have known is really mine, stored away in the subconscious quality of myself; why should I spend time in vain regrets that I may not travel to meet the oriole's call when it is forever imbedded in the vast storehouse of my memory? The quality of my youthful observation hypnotized me into the understanding that the simple ways of God's other creatures were good for me too. Twilight brought home the birds to squabble and argue out the day's ill will—or good fortune. Night came and gave them sleep and aroused the furry brothers from their drowsy days. All hurts and harm and fears were eventually adjusted in the processes of living, weariness and terror were lost in peace and rest. Tomorrow always brought another program of adventure.

Individuation is the doorway to the universal. The secret of it is to live one's Self, one's own life, to be what one is. There is no natural law that says I must confine myself to the present experience of the senses. I am not thus confined in fact, because my nature knows immensely wider freedoms. And if I neglect these wider freedoms—sweet memories and high imagination—I surrender up to nothingness great segments of my birthright.

Lay this book aside a moment, then, relax in mind and body, and recall one of the loveliest experiences of your life. Bring it forth out of the past—time is no barrier—and out of whatever distance—space is no barrier, either—recover its qualities, all of its qualities, as vividly as you can; and seeing the picture of it in your mind, feeling the thrill of emotional response to its appeal, live once again in that high moment of happiness and delight. Know within yourself that you have a legitimate right to be released into the joy that exists beyond the senses.

Having practiced the little exercise I have suggested, if you will now examine, quite rationally, the particular episode which you recalled out of the past, you will have a clue to your own inner quality and nature. For if the experience was lovely to you, you have only to compare it with the usual current activities of your life to see whether or not you are reasonably fulfilling your destiny and nature. If you are not—and most people are not—then you will have received your first lesson in deeper sensory values, and accordingly you can proceed, in some measure at least, with the management of your life.

Psychologists will call such practices "escapes from reality" perhaps; and they *are* escapes—not *from* reality, but into it. Is it more "real" for me to see the motor car today, to hear its horn and smell the poisonous stench of its exhaust, than it is to revisit in imagination a sunlit beach I know on the Riviera, with the blue Mediterranean reaching away into the distance, and behind me a lovely hill dotted with gardens and cool villas where people, many of them my friends, once lived beautifully? To recover all this I now have to go back into the past of time, as well as to distant France; but in doing so I bring up into awareness a group of stimuli vastly different from the sight and sound and smell of the automobile; and in consequence I live, for a few moments at least, re-immersed in happiness, faith, and the devotions that are basic in my own being.

That whole happy past, revived in consciousness, evokes a present sadness, because war has disrupted those ample ways of living; but that sadness deepens the quality of the memory, and the past and the present have thus enriched each other *in me*.

Why should we not practice a good technique of escape? Those who specialize in the study of abnormalities have found that "escape mechanisms" are conducive to fixed states of delusion and permanent dissociations. Personally, I don't think this is the root of the matter. I believe such conditions to be symptoms and not causes, and it is to be noted that capable psychiatrists are daily bringing people back to normal by going to the roots of such difficulties. A good escape mechanism may mean salvation from the nervous strains of life; and as a matter of fact, we all indulge in them more or less. Someone has said that we go to sleep when we become tired of ourselves; but such a statement can apply only to people who have not learned how consciously to escape into the supersensory areas of their own existence.

I discovered for myself the basic values of such escapes years ago, when I was at the British College of Psychic Science. Because people came there for sittings, I often went into trance three times a day, in endeavors to give them some communication from "the world of spirit." And not infrequently, under the impact of the shabby personality and the maudlin sentimentality of these visitors, I was glad to escape into the trance condition—into a state of psychological, spiritual freedom—away from the weight and drag which some people imposed on my senses and my nervous sensibilities. It was often obvious that as personalities these people were incapable and unworthy of brave, deep devotion; I knew beyond question that they could only be a strain upon the energies of the entities whom they sought to "contact"; and since I then had a growing belief in the rights of the dead to their peace, I sometimes suffered a spasm of rebellion and self-distaste at the necessity which made me the instrument of these inadequate appeals to their attention.

Actually, we all want passionately to *live*, though many of us have forgotten what living means. Basically it means experiencing—experiencing the strong active play of our own vital forces—not as vicarious responses to somebody else's exploits, as in reading a book, watching a football game or a play in the theatre, but in direct response to, direct identification with, the circumstances, events, and personalities that have immediate and pressing consequences for our existence or for the maintenance of our individual integrity.

Yet consider how vicariously most of us do live. Holding safely to a job as the basis of our existence, we spend most of our lives in habitual and routine activities. To escape from the ennui of such dull habits, we find material for our *interest* in the newspaper, the radio, or the movies. Generally speaking, and for most of us, "entertainment" consists in that escape from the flatness of our own lives which can be secured with the least trouble and the least expense.

We all want passionately to live, yet few of us live passionately. Why is this so? What is it that is missing from the formulae of our lives? Stimulus. We have become so accustomed to depending on our five senses for the stimuli to our experience in this world that we have all but forgotten that within our very selves lie the sources of our outer experience—or the lack of it. Many of us have become completely lost in the activities of the collective psyche, and the only evidences of individualism that we feel or express consist in our personality responses to what *happens* to come to our attention.

But we can live creatively from our own centers, if we really wish to do so. Within each one of us there is the long history of our racial and personal past. Do we know the content of our subconscious? Most of us do not. And within each one of us there wait the faculties for testing the measureless future of both time and space. Are we aware of these faculties? Most of us are not. But we can become active in both of these additional fields of consciousness if we wish. If that is the case, we shall find ourselves also living more realistically and more interestingly—more vitally—at the levels of sensory experience.

I am not suggesting that large numbers of people shall attempt to become "psychic," but I am suggesting—even recommending—that they take some steps toward an awareness of the supersensory areas of the human being.

I have already suggested an excursion into the happiness of memory, and I have intimated a possible extension of perception beyond the obvious sensory field. In addition I should like to suggest, for the experimentation of anyone who may be interested, that he pause again and ask himself what sure knowledge he possesses concerning tomorrow—the tomorrow of his own personal life. He will probably see himself getting started in the morning—breakfast, and so on, as usual, and he can preview a certain number of engagements and activities that will fill most of his day. But in each of these activities and engagements is he sure of the outcome? Is he even sure of what he wants the outcome to be? On mature consideration does he know the ends and purposes he wants to serve? And finally, are these aims and purposes his own or somebody else's business?

Men and women living in the modern world are entitled, by the quality of their natural endowments, to some measure of assurance relative to their own destinies—not only for tomorrow, but for much further reaches of future time also. Committed as we all are to collective activities, we can nevertheless find such assurances concerning our private fate, if we will look within ourselves—where questions and problems repeatedly arise and are repeatedly determined.

What I am writing here must not be superficially thought of as a basis for some kind of a "success" technique. On the contrary, it carries no promise of "success," in the sense in which we commonly understand that word. But it suggests a new realism for both "successful" and unsuccessful people—for all those who have the courage to attempt to become individuals—for all those within whom the impulse to individualism stirs. What profiteth it a man if he gain the whole world and lose his own soul? The innate qualities of one's self have come into existence for the purpose of being amplified and fulfilled. Happy is the man who finds the means for expressing himself in his work, and in his work gains the means to his personal freedom. A good many of us have "big jobs" to do, and do them efficiently, yet never find the time to note how far, in our success, we have failed to be ourselves. There are a good many "individualists" abroad in the world who have completely lost contact with their own individuality. That unique fragment of universal and eternal being, which has been fashioned by the ages, is not to be discovered in the outer areas of sensory perception, but by the exercise of the supersensory faculties with which we are all endowed.

These pages are meant only to be suggestive. They may contain a certain manifestation of hypnotic action. But in sending this "magnetism" out into the world, one can only wonder mildly what its effect may be. One does not have to know precisely, for one does not mean to control the dissociations, perceptions (true or false), and activities of the reader. All that one has to be sure of is one's clear honesty of statement and one's clear honesty of purpose in making the statement. On these points I have satisfied myself. I write from the assurance of my own experience. And the purpose? The purpose is to free, by however much or little, the consciousness of mankind, now unnecessarily restricted by fear of itself—fear of the power and splendor of man's own innate capacities. Since this fear is the effect of man's self-hypnosis, induced by his relations to the sensory world, its cure lies in self-hypnosis of a different kind. And if we *will*, we can overcome that fear with courage; for the cultivation of the *will* is perhaps the highest psychological process possible to self-hypnosis.

IV
Dissociation and Awareness

IN HUMAN PSYCHOLOGY, and behind awareness, there move numerous intangible forces, electric in quality, which are the results of the transmutation by the organism of all those factors which enter into that synthetic sum which is the synthetic individual. Some of these forces are continuously active, as long as life inhabits the human corpus—sensory perception, some measure of emotional and nervous response, thought or fantasy, and the operation of metabolism in the organism. But awareness does not commonly reach every level at which these forces are at work. Though awareness may be filled with the content of the subconscious at times and at will, it has relatively little concern with those areas so ancient and so largely automatic. Awareness is always concerned with the present. Even when the mind reaches into the past, into the future, and into distances of space, awareness occurs only here and now.

As I have said, sleep is a normal psychological condition in which awareness, the synthetic crown of personality, becomes quiescent and inactive, because of dissociation. In our normal waking state various stimuli are constantly affecting consciousness by way of the five senses, keeping the cerebrum in a state of mild excitation and the cerebral neurons more or less charged with nervous energy. When we go to sleep, our thoughts and our reception of sensory stimuli are decreased in number and vigor, the cerebral activity subsides, the energy ebbs in the cerebral neurons, the brain comes to rest, and sensory stimuli affect only the lower nervous levels—the subconscious.

Are such changes of condition sufficient to warrant us in dividing consciousness into the two parts of the subconscious and the conscious? I think they are. And the separation of the third part of consciousness, which I have called the superconscious, is equally warranted by other differences which occur in these same areas of stimuli, cerebral activity, and the energy of the neurons.

If sleep, which is a subnormal, subconscious condition (relative to our normal waking life), occurs through the subsidence of our reception of and our response to stimuli, then states which can be called supernormal or superconscious (relative to our normal waking life) must be marked by some intensification of stimuli and of nervous and cerebral response.

And this is so. The whole theory of the superconscious is based in the idea of concentration—a concentration of the entire psychological set-up, including expectancy, attention, desire, will, and action, upon a given superpersonal purpose. Just as we sink away in sleep into the relaxation of a subconscious condition which may be thought of as negative, so in superconscious experiences we achieve a new focus and tension of all the faculties of our life, and by this concentration of the life-forces upon levels of consciousness that transcend both the subconscious and the conscious, we come into new fields of perception, awareness, and knowledge.

Without being too technical, it will perhaps be interesting if a key to the meaning of dissociation is given here. The following indicative paragraph is quoted from the *Encyclopedia Britannica.*[*]

> In the normal state of the brain, when any idea is present to consciousness, the corresponding neural disposition is in a state of dominant excitement, but the intensity of that excitement is moderated, depressed or partially inhibited by the sub-excitement of many rival or competing dispositions of other systems with which it is connected. Suppose now that all the nervous connections between the multitudinous dispositions of the cerebrum are by some means rendered less effective, that the association-paths are partially blocked or functionally depressed; the result will be that, while the most intimate connections, those between dispositions of any one system, remain functional and permeable, the weaker less intimate connections, those between dispositions belonging to different systems, will be practically abolished for the time being; each system of dispositions will then function more or less as an isolated system, and its activity will no longer be subject to the depressing or inhibiting influence of other systems; therefore each system, on being excited in any way, will tend to its end with more than normal force, being freed from all interferences; that is to say, each idea or system of ideas will tend to work itself out and realize itself in action immediately, without suffering the opposition of antagonistic ideas which, in the normal state of the brain, might altogether prevent its realization in action.

Dissociation, thus briefly indicated, is a psychological theory of primary importance. At the moment, psychology takes a general position that dissociation is "abnormal"; but this attitude is of course based on the study of abnormal psychological cases. My own opinion is that in abnormal cases

* *Encyclopedia Britannica* (1910), s. v. "Hypnotism."

dissociation is a symptom and not a cause, the cause lying far deeper in the individual psyche than the dissociation theory reaches. Dissociation may be either normal or abnormal, according to its actual expressive value in life; and the key to the difference is to be found in the fact—whether the dissociation is a tool or means for the purposive and creative release of the psyche, or whether it dominates and limits the life of the individual. In either case, the psychic nature is at the root of the factual condition, is the pressure-point of either the "normal" or the "abnormal" expression and experience.

Actually, dissociation is a condition essential to the achievement of all our best creative activities. One of the reasons why more of us are not more creative is that we are not yet capable of establishing the conditions of selective dissociation within our psychological selves. No important concentration upon a given theme is accomplished without a temporary dissociation; the ability to achieve such selective dissociations is a mark of high psychological quality and integration; it is fostered by our whole educational system, and it is the goal of all our scientific and business efficiency.

What is fundamentally involved is the power selectively to direct the psychic forces. But the psyche will not be controlled beyond a certain point, and conditions of abnormal dissociation differ from normal dissociations in this: they are over-concentrations of the consciousness upon the self, due to an egoic conflict between some deep need of the psyche and a failure to release (sometimes by forceful inhibition) that need's expression.

In such cases we have a return to a primitive state of consciousness that lies in the long gap between animal instinct and the civilized mind. The key to this primitive condition is the identification of the self with all objective phenomena—all that it perceives is intimately related to *it*; while the mark of true civilized cultures is their capacity for differentiating perceptions into countless degrees of relationship, intimate and remote.

In the first chapter of this book I referred to man's capacity for impersonal objective perception as the crown of his uniqueness. In the pursuit and achievement of impersonal objective perceptions, man has to learn the processes of selective dissociation, including the capacity to transcend the sensory field; but the maintenance of the human norm depends not only upon the individual's capacity to be thus selective, but also upon his continuing ability to release himself from such selective concentrations and to reestablish the variety of his associational relationships.

Here, as elsewhere, we have a pair of opposites—association and dissociation. These words stand as general names for two human capacities. Between them, in the individual case, stands consciousness, selecting and rejecting, according to its present quality, among the various data that reach it perceptively. Much of its selectivity is unconscious and habitual—an almost purely subconscious activity. But if and when one becomes declarative, instead of being merely receptive of life, one unites the two capacities of association and dissociation in a more or less positive and independent undertaking.

At such a time one concentrates, as we say. Much of such concentration consists in the withdrawal of attention from the sensory field, and in its centralization upon the content of the consciousness at some other psychic level. If successful, such concentration on the content of the consciousness is, as a process, truly creative. But since man can create disastrously as well as constructively, the qualitative value achieved by the concentration depends upon the psychic qualities that are dominant in the particular creative process.

Whether "good" or "bad," such achievements affect the subconscious, building up there, in their measure, the quality of the individual nature and status. Selfish and self-centered concentrations may be said to be of an in-growing type; they are reactionary in the sense that they tend to crystallize about themselves, and thus inhibit the freedom of the psyche. It will be obvious how the fears and oddities of psychological "cases" eventuate in consequence. They are divisive and isolationist. But those concentrations which are truly "objective" and impersonal—that are concerned with realities beyond the individual—expand the consciousness and release the psyche into wider fields of experience. They amount to the temporary sacrifice of the consciousness to the psyche; but the consciousness is always rewarded.

Our word "concentration" is allied to the idea of "concentric": having a common center, as a series of circles, one within another, all based on a common central point. I conceive such a concentric figure as a symbol of constructive concentration; it is integrated in fact, yet there is no limit to the areas possible of inclusion within it, through the addition of other circles, either within or without the form. But the center on which the whole figure—and the whole process—is based, while it is the very core of the psychological subjective, must nevertheless be objective to the consciousness. Sound concentration is always the attempt of the consciousness to identify itself with something that lies just beyond the reach of its present apprehension, perception, or comprehension. Concentration and contemplation consist in the focusing of consciousness upon a center which is central to itself, yet objective to it—as the center is to the periphery of a circle.

The secret to the difference between "good" and "bad" dissociation lies in the particular centralization that is achieved. In concentration a mysterious dual psychological effect eventuates: the psychic quality is intensified, while the consciousness acquires a firmer integration with that center. It consequently makes a vast difference whether the concentration is objective or not.

In the chapter on "Symbolism" I refer to one of my own symbols, a bright spiral, which is a signal of my capacity to do clairvoyant work. Watching this bright spiral, always in movement, curve within curve, and with its point, the center of all the curves and circles, forever moving outward into spaceless distance, I have felt and I know how the quality of consciousness is modified by concentration on the objective center. I am speaking here of a symbol which represents the fact. The ever-receding point of the spiral is not itself the center, but the whole figure is like a form in electrical imagery, set up to focus the qualitative psychological process which is itself wholly immaterial. The candle flame of the contemplative and the crystal ball of the seer are similarly set up to lead consciousness into the abstract.

All types of concentration are based in dissociation. In a certain sense, and from the general present point of view, all dissociations are "abnormal." But in my opinion, this concept does not represent a final perception, and I have no doubt that—probably in the near future—psychology will find, through the dissociation theory, new keys to the realities of man's psychic life. Meanwhile, the differences between the effects which are created by "good" and "bad" dissociations may be tentatively discriminated by an examination of the aims and purposes of individual concentrations of consciousness.

The quality of our dissociations depends upon the quality of our natures—not on the *fundamental* quality of them, but on that part which is perceptive and expressive in the present condition or status of the consciousness. There is no man who cannot transcend himself. Yet most of us do not commonly transcend ourselves, because we have not yet developed a curiosity in the subjective fields of awareness. Supersensory activities involve dissociation; but these activities are normal because they are free and expansive, and they consequently differ from dissociations that are dominant and inhibitory as day differs from night—and that is a very good simile to sum up the whole theme.

Human life is full of fantasy. As a life-process, and considered as a whole, it operates for everyone alike; yet no two individualized consciousnesses can be exactly alike, so for each one of us fantasy is a separate and special performance acted out on the stage of the subconscious. In these performances each one of us has the center of the stage and does as he wills or wishes.

This willing and wishing represent the very stuff of our most private existence. For each one of us fantasy may become a key to the realities of the future, provided we bring the substance of it into conscious understanding and action.

What, then, does fantasy mean to *me*? It represents the world I have to live in—the world which I myself, being what I am, make out of the facts, events, and possibilities of life. For me personally, because I have brought up much of the fundamental fantasy of my life into the areas of awareness, the subjective holds no fears. It is, instead, at the root of a love of living, which

I constantly feel, and it is the spring that waters the tree of a great curiosity about life. This curiosity and this love of living I believe to be aspects of a dynamism which has been developed through the integration of the parts of my consciousness into a working unity. To arrive at this unity I have suffered consciously, have dared to invade the deep subconscious, and have discovered certain areas of the superconscious. Our fear of the unknown subconscious is really the symbol of our fear of Life. Most of us fear the impact of our innate energies as we might fear the pressure of a terrific tonnage on our bodies.

What we have to learn to do is to extend the faculty of awareness into both the subconscious and the superconscious areas of the natural universe. As in our individual lives, the universal life is the present effect or result of the age-old operation of natural laws. In these ancient processes changes have occurred in the universe, and other changes are constantly occurring. It is the nature of the finite human mind to split this continuous process into parts, and so we think of the past, the present, and the future; but to conceive life and the universe as a continuous and timeless process, like a seamless garment, is to take the first step out of the relative isolation of our individualism and into that universality of consciousness which is man's highest affinity and capacity.

Personally, I do not consider "psychism" in any of its aspects as an end in itself, but as a means to fuller living. "Here" and "there"—whatever one may conceive these words to mean—the governors of life are the same; and it is the privilege of the human consciousness to discover this vital fact. In super-sensory activities one holds out a hand to heaven; and, as in Michelangelo's symbolic painting, "Creation of Man," the divine life of the whole floods the human being with new vitality, elan, and awareness. One sees visions and dreams, dreams that carry one beyond the confines of oneself, and the purposes of one's little life begin to partake of universalistic qualities. One begins to judge life and the world, not prejudicially, but with an increasing sense of the reality of *things as they are.*

Ultimately, the value of psychic experience, for the individual, lies in the fact that it releases the human consciousness into its full affinity with the great life. To transmute the unknown into form and meaning is to live, in some measure, at one with eternity.

There seems to exist a general impression that in undertaking supersensory activities one mysteriously goes off by oneself into areas of consciousness and experience which are superhuman, or at least somehow inhuman. Of course this is not so. One may take whatever view of psychic activities one wishes, the fact remains that whatever the human individual experiences and expresses is pertinent to the human psyche. In such experiences one is never isolated, never alone. The human consciousness can participate only in the fields of consciousness as a whole; but there is no known limit to the fields of consciousness, and there is no known limit to the possible participation of the finite human consciousness in these infinite fields.

Going into the superconscious field corresponds very largely with going into the subconscious field. If we attempt to evoke the memory of a past event, for instance, our success depends upon the recovery of images out of "the past." (But where is the past?) Such images may be replicas of people, places, activities, circumstances, events. And drawing these symbolic images together, out of space-time and into our present awareness, we re-create, according to our capacity, a wholly immaterial, non-sensory episode. Moreover, the re-created form may have such force and value that we are again emotionally and mentally stirred by it as we were by the factual occurrence of which it is a reproduction. In these recoveries we are never alone, but always accompanied by the people and conditions of the memory; but the psychological *values* of such a recovery depend upon what we make of the whole event.

When one enters the supersensory field of the unknown, one follows a psychological technique which corresponds in many ways with the operation of memory. One consciously makes his approach, symbolic forms appear out of space-time—and these forms mean something to the consciousness that perceives them. *What* they mean depends upon that consciousness. But interpreting them according to its quality and capacity, the consciousness evokes an immaterial image in awareness. And as in the case of memory, so here, the prototypes which thus become significant in our present awareness affect the organism emotionally and mentally, and the subconscious is further enriched by the experience.

The difference between the two processes of recalling or remembering and experiencing in the superconscious is, of course, the fact that in remembering we are partially reproducing in awareness something previously experienced, while in clairvoyance, for instance, we are perceiving something which has not been previously experienced *by the perceiving consciousness.* The key to the result, in both cases, seems to me to be the *awareness.* Each supersensory perception, including recall, constitutes a new thing in awareness.

Where has the experience of all the past of all human lives gone? Where does the world-wide experience of this present moment come from? and where will it go? Is not the entire activity of tomorrow already prepared and patterned? And is not our awareness steadily approaching those facts and activities as the clock ticks off the minutes? Do I actually have to wait upon the clock? Things are occurring in the universe now of which no human consciousness is aware. Where is this place in which everything occurs, regardless of the consciousness of man? It is everywhere, of course, both in space and time, and only our materialistic training prevents us from grasping a clearer perception of the whole.

To me, the various activities of remembering the past, thinking of something distant in the present—the Sphinx, for instance, or a picture that hangs on my wall in another room and is not present to sight —preparing the program of tomorrow's activities, and entering upon a superconscious experience—all of these involve the activity of conscious awareness in various supersensory distances of space-time. If we watch closely to see how these activities occur within ourselves, we may discover, for each and all of them, a sensation of concentration in the forebrain. And in such watching we shall also discover that, as a part of the process, the breathing has been quieted.

Awareness is the identification of the individual consciousness with something that is objective to itself. Many things are constantly happening to us which are duly registered in the subconscious, but which do not affect awareness. And many other things do affect awareness, but only in a relatively unimportant way. But the volitional projections of awareness in identifications with objective data are creative activities of a positive and determining kind, and such experiences are all similar in type, whether they deal with the past, the present, or the future.

Such volitional projections of awareness originate in whatever psychic phase may be dominant in the personality at the time—physical, emotional, mental, and so forth—and our free development, through experience, normally consists in a process in which consciousness is constantly taking the next step forward in its natural development.

Awareness thus becomes our psychic focus; and when it occurs as a free process we have a progressive fulfilling of the psychic nature. All about us spreads space-time, measureless and everlasting, filled with the constant activities of forms without number—all invisible as in a great darkness. By means of awareness, set up like a lighthouse on the coast of human consciousness, and casting its beam abroad, we discern fragments of being and movement in the great darkness. To the west, the light uncovers the past (recall); to the south, it reveals the immediate factual present (sensory perception); to the east, it brings out things existing in the present, but beyond the sensory reach (memory); to the north, it penetrates into the future (planning, imagination, contemplation, superconscious perception). The genius of man consists in the fact that he possesses this searchlight of awareness, and that he is finally learning to understand the unity of the whole field in which it operates.

V
The Breath and Color

THE BREATH MAY PERHAPS be said to be the most essential element for human existence at the physical level. Everything on this earth is somehow affected by the atmosphere. When present, the breath does extraordinary things to the human organism; in its absence extraordinary things happen to the organism also. When the human being can no longer breathe, he dies, and his synthetic physical structure disintegrates into its various elements.

We commonly think of the breath—when we think of it at all—as our inhalation and exhalation of the atmosphere; but the atmosphere is a compound substance, and in breathing we unconsciously separate its ingredients, taking in those that we want and rejecting others. There are people who become conscious and expert in this selective breathing. We are all familiar with the necessity of excluding carbon-monoxide from our lungs, and we often hold our breathing suspended until we are able to escape from the zone of atmosphere thus poisoned. We are all familiar too with the pleasure of inhaling the fresh smell of the sea, the scent of pine woods, and the perfume of flowers. But for the most part, our breathing is but one aspect of our subconscious life.

Being basic to human life, the breath is an instrument of vitality, a conveyor of life itself. Like many other factors in our customary living—diet, exercise, medication—it is an instrument the usefulness of which may be enhanced by means of intelligent experimentation and development. For simple physical health we are taught to breathe deeply; the management of the breath is an important part of all techniques of elocution and singing. We use it for our ordinary speech, and it is thus one of the principal instruments for our self-expression.

From our usual experience in breath control—in singing and other particular techniques—we have a basic recognition of the fact and the effectiveness of manipulation of the breath. And in the yogic practices of the East, as we know, breath control is a fundamental factor. The manipulations of breath control may be, and are, used to induce dissociation. This is readily understandable. The breath and the rate of breathing directly affect the blood flow in the human organism; the blood flow, strong and pure, or weak and impure, determines the organism's vital quality (life-force), which affects the nervous system and its efficiency, and thus differentiates the capacity or tone of its sentiency (consciousness).

Our English word "animate" comes from the Latin *animare*: to fill with breath; and many of our conscious methods of breath control consist precisely in the process of animating certain sections of our being by filling them with the breath in certain ways.

In my own approach to the conditions of telepathy, control of the breath is the first step. Not only the lungs are involved in this breathing, but the diaphragm; and below the diaphragm there follows an effect—as though an immaterial essence of the breath somehow operates in my system in ways which are not familiar to physical science or to the physical senses. Sentiency is involved in the process, for I become aware—aware of symbols, of the solar plexus, and of subtle movements within my body, like the most delicate flowing of energy over allied nerve systems; and of course I know, from long and minute self examination, that these are factual occurrences, not effects of imagination.

The solar plexus is described as a great network of nerves and sympathetic ganglia that lies back of the stomach and distributes nervous impulses to the intestines, stomach, and glands in the upper part of the abdominal cavity. It is thus allied to the subconscious; and that I become aware of the solar plexus in these special breathing exercises would seem to mean that the breathing process transfers the focus of consciousness from the conscious to the subconscious field. But awareness does not stop and stay in these phases of delicate sensation. It is only because I have been sufficiently interested, in a scientific sense, to examine the whole process as meticulously as possible, that I am able to speak of the stimulating effect of the breathing upon the solar plexus area. I have no doubt, however, that a particular controlled rhythm of breathing does affect the usual metabolism of the organism, and that certain delicate effects of the change of which one becomes aware are not imaginatively produced, but result from the shift of awareness to unusual regions of sensation thus stimulated.

Under these circumstances sensations flow in two directions, upward and downward, in my body. How much of this sense of downward flow may be caused by electrical energies moving to ground I do not know. Privately, I think of this phase as still the operation of the breath. But this sense of downward movement is not caused by delicate sensation only; it is accompanied by its own symbolism; and one of the most common of these symbols is in the form of an inverted lily, with its stem emerging from the nerve plexus and the mouth of its bell pointing downward.

From my earliest encounter with the symbolic tree of life so commonly represented in Eastern rugs and pictures, I understood it perfectly, accepting it in the most natural way. Not until I was mature did I have occasion to discover that it is usually thought of as a clever imaginative idea of metaphysical estheticism. Actually, I have no doubt that it originated in a valid psychic perception. At any rate, in my own mind, there is a constant correspondence between the symbolic tree of life and my own symbol of the inverted lily which I apprehend as stemming out of the solar plexus.

I never have any sense of the return of the energy that flows downward; but I have said that sensation flows in two major directions, and that which flows upward from the solar plexus rises in curves within the frontal surfaces of my torso, moves across the shoulders, and returns to the solar plexus region by way of the spine.

What is this energy that moves in circling sensation in my body? Frankly, I do not know. But my inner sense of its movement is much more positive than my sense of the movement of the blood in my arteries and veins. It is as though a new process of metabolism were temporarily set up in my body. And I say "temporarily" because I am aware of its occurrence only as an effect of special breathing, and then but briefly, for awareness presently becomes concerned with other things. Nevertheless, I have a clear inner picture of this process of movement as a whole. It is a somewhat complex three-way movement, indescribable in words, but possible of indication in a symbolic pattern which I have attempted to reproduce.

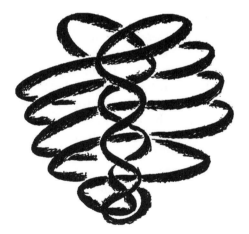

Considered as a symbol, and reduced to its simplest terms, this figure might be thought of as a three-dimensional variation on the two-dimensional theme of the caduceus of Hermes, the third dimension being, of course, a factor of vital movement in the present case. Yet it is interesting to recall that in the Kundalini yoga, the mysterious Serpent Fire, in its three aspects (Ida, feminine; Pingala, masculine; Sushumna, the united), is also said to develop on lines symbolically corresponding to the caduceus.

These are interesting side-lights on my impression of the sensations which develop as one of the effects of special breathing. I mention the correspondences in passing because, if one cares to consider them, they suggest that the sensations I have mentioned (while these are purely personal to myself, so far as I know) may have very ancient and very deep significances in the whole process of psychic development.

As I have said, this is a process which is deliberately set up. I become aware of it but for a moment. And in the same moment, as I have learned by careful watching, consciousness escapes from its centralization in the sensory field, and a supersensory process begins.

To the best of my knowledge and belief, supersensory perception (in telepathy or clairvoyance, for instance) does not commonly consist, as some people seem to think, in a direct flight of consciousness to some privileged point of vantage where one can hear and see and know the particular experience which one is seeking. It is not a process like memory or imagination, in which, if I choose, I can transfer awareness to the Capitol at Washington or can again pass along the Champs Elysées in Paris. Unquestionably there are many experiences of ample and direct perception of a psychic kind, such as those recorded by Mr. Harold M. Sherman, in *Thoughts Through Space*, and my own experience in the "Newfoundland Experiment," which I have reported elsewhere.* But *these* types of supernormal activity involve the whole range of one's super-sensory capacities, including clairvoyance, telepathy, clairaudience, and precognition.

Much supersensory perception is accomplished, however, by processes of watching and waiting in the consciousness. One *sees* lines and colors and symbols. These move, and one is wholly concentrated on them and their movement. I say "symbols" here for want of a better word. I frequently see curving lines of light and color that flow forward in strata, and in these strips or ribbons of movement there will appear other sharply angled lines that form and change and fade like arrow heads aimed and passing in various directions. And in this flow of energy that is full of form and color, these arrow heads will presently indicate the letter H. Each line of the H will be an independent curve, and their combination will not remain identifiable for very long. But I shall have caught it; and holding it suspended in awareness, I continue to watch the process develop and unfold. Soon a rapidly drifting A appears in the field of concentration, and then, let us suppose, an R; and presently I have gathered the word HARRY out of the void, either as a proper name or as a verb temporarily without either subject or object. Whether it is actually noun or verb will depend upon the context of the perception as a whole.

This process is infinitely rapid. But I have achieved an alertness of attention, of awareness, of being, which is equal to this rapid flow of immaterial line and color and symbol, and out of this alertness, poised above the flow-

---

* In Eileen J. Garrett (1939). *My Life as the Search for the Meaning of Mediumship.* New York: Oquaga Press.

ing stream of differentiated energy, I gather a message with a meaning—a message which has come to my consciousness out of the objective world as factually as the reflected light from the distant Moon may reach my consciousness by way of my sense of sight.

In such conditions one hears as one sees—if one hears at all. But clairvoyance and clairaudience are differentiated from each other, just as sight and sound are differentiated in the sensory field. And what differentiates them for supersensory perception, exactly as in the sensory field, is the nature of the stimuli which affect some inner capacity of perception—neither eye nor ear—whose sensitivity becomes operative through processes of dissociation.

To me, the solar plexus is a vital center of first importance. It almost seems as though the organism were separated into two parts, upper and lower, by the diaphragm. I have become aware of this subtle division through sensations of feeling and sensations of color, sensations which are at times sensorily perceived; and the first step toward the origination of these perceptions and sensations is the deep manipulation of the breath.

I conceive the solar plexus to be the womb of color. Those sensations which I think of as flowing downward from this center, and which give the effect of possible electric energies moving to ground, constitute the spectrum of the grays, so to say—for between pure black and pure white there is a color-range of grays the "values" of which are as varied as the values of red, yellow, and blue.

I can conceive these gray tones only as negative, for they are at first sight unobtrusive; yet they turn back on themselves as though to produce darker tones out of deeper being, and they are at times lovely in their impressionistic purity. Relative to the reds that crowd and glow at the solar plexus itself, however, they quickly fade out of one's general impression—having waked the deeper tones, as it were. The reds are vigorous, almost violent at times, and not always beautiful. One feels (though not emotionally) a tremendous power in them. And drawing or driving this power upward in one's body to the nameless place where consciousness is centered, one unfolds a kaleidoscopic flood of color within oneself. Does this actually occur as a process, as it seems to, in one's physical organism? This I know: it is accomplished by means of the rhythmic downward pressure of the breath into the vicinity of the solar plexus.

Below the radiance of the red lies the deeper purple, ranging upward into lavender and crystal shades, on which the rays of healing are carried. The breath we breathe carries the whole chemistry of color. According to *our* nature and quality, it finds its own depth and level in each human individual being, and there transforms itself chemically into strength, healing light, and energy. It is my experience that all healing for others is carried out on the rays that run from deepest tones of purple to the lavenders and beautiful opaline shades that in time give place to the deep yellows of the spiritual consciousness. Green is the color of health. It mixes and radiates as within an inner mechanism, blending itself with light, until it returns at last into the soft bright radiance which is the basic "substance" of the whole experience.

In these experiences of inner color-process one has a feeling, an impression, a sense, of freedom and expansion which I can only describe as corresponding to the feeling that we have in body and senses when we are fully at one with nature—field, hedgerow, sky, flowers, trees, and running water.

Every breath we draw is an expression of our *unconscious* desire to participate in the activities of the life-principle. Is it not obvious that in a *conscious* attempt to participate more deeply in life we shall surely succeed? The man who refuses to be caught by the adventure around the corner of space-time does not know the value of breathing the breath of life. I know this for myself, for there have been times when I have cried out against living. The serious asthmatic illness that I suffered, with the break-down of the lungs, I traced back to a fear of life that was engendered in my very early youth. The breath, in my estimation, is our most natural, unconscious participation in the universal existence; it our prayer of unity with life, an act of faith, a magic potion by which we are allied to the will to live; and our exhalations, in thought, word, and action, bear the magic of our tiny contribution to the quality of the whole. The breath is our eternal love-life with Omnipotence.

Alas, that we have not all known this from the beginning! The dancer and the singer have had to learn it. Our army of youth is now learning how the breath decides the issues of life and death. Men drive ships of steel through the sky, above the cities and mountains, and others maintain themselves in the bowels of ships beneath the surface of the sea. Does it mean nothing to the universal, nothing to human destiny, that the armies of the air and the ocean depths are becoming familiar with oxygen and with breath control?

We know that the human body is composed of myriads of tiny organisms, each one living a life of its own within its own universe—which is the individual human being in whose body it has its place. How many and what "events" affect these tiny lives? In a corresponding way, each human being is a tiny organism, living its own life in the immense universe of eternal space-time. We all know that we are dependent upon and definitely affected by mysterious operations in the universe at large and by such matters as the changing weathers of our planet's atmosphere. In the cold and darkness of winter, in our temperate zone, we suffer a restriction and contraction of the freedom of our lives. And as the sun moves northward again, and winter gives way to spring, and spring to summer, we expand, exposing our bodies to the play of sunshine and genial airs, and shattering the restrictive chrysalis of our winter routines. I surmise that in special breathing processes, such as those to which I have referred, we create a private summer season for many of the countless lives that constitute our bodies, and free them from the constrictions of our usual unconcern. In this freedom their vitality is enhanced and expanded, and they emanate a vital force which takes on a phenomenal aspect for those who perceive it.

In my own psychic work I am repeatedly aware of sensations of movement within my body, such as I have attempted to describe. These are not sensations of physical movement only. Rather do they seem to be movements within the vitality of the nerves, as subtle as the blood-flow or the movement of thought. Is it too much to suggest that the fresh vitalization of cell and nerve structures, creating an amplification of the vital force of myriads of cells in one's body, is the source of these "unsubstantiated" sensations?

The cell is known to be an individual life-form, capable of nourishment, reproduction, and so on. And I have no doubt that it is out of some process of the fusion of such tiny emanations that the superior and mysterious essence of the human consciousness is evolved. To grasp the realism of this idea, we have to remember that these little lives possess no sensory capacities, no capacities of selectivity; but each and all, they do possess a fundamental vitality and a particular quality of their own, and they live as they can—as they must. But if the fused sum of their emanations could turn in upon itself (as consciousness can), and if by virtue of its synthetic superiority it could discover objective means for stimulating the elements of its own content, a whole series of developmental circles would then ensue *for consciousness,* and theories of evolution would become problems in particular techniques of human activity—in which breathing would undoubtedly be fundamental.

For myself, I know that the vitality of the human organism is a synthesis of energies which are being constantly received, transformed, fused, and expressed by the organism. No two people are, or can be, alike; yet the countless differentiations of quality that exist among us all are the results of a single process which is fundamental to human beings, a process in which we individually participate, either more or less deeply.

This whole process, as it works itself out in the life of any man, becomes the synthetic *quality* of his life, the quality of his synthetic consciousness as a whole. And I have *seen* this essence of the nature of an individual withdraw from the physical body, as one sees his own exhaled breath on a frosty morning.

And contemplating the withdrawal of this mysterious emanation from the organism, I have thought of it as the final out-breathing of that particular lifecycle—the end of a phase which, as I observed the phenomenon, impressed my consciousness with the assurance of its further relationship and continuity in the universal life.

In our Western civilization we have largely centered our attention upon the development of the rational mind at the sensory level, and our science has become definitely materialistic. The common criticism which the West makes of the East is that it is too "mystical"—not materialistic enough. But conversely, the East criticizes the West for excessive materialism. Probably both points of view are correct. In the present world war we have become aware that East and West can see eye to eye on fundamental issues, and that neither the evil nor the good in human existence is confined to either hemisphere. India, China, and Japan, in the East, have given three radically different exhibitions of human behavior in recent years, as France, Great Britain, and Germany have given in the West. It is evident that civilization has nowhere achieved a norm. In all civilized cultures there has existed—up to the present time—a tendency to crystallization. Patterns tend to become fixed, inhibiting further expansion. Such crystallizations, when they occur, inevitably have to be broken, because as they congeal they tend to cramp the freedom of the life-force by reducing human consciousness to the levels of particularities—preciousness and minutiae.

It is not the nature of either the life-force or consciousness to tolerate restriction, however, for both are qualified to the universal pattern. In the West we have still to realize—though we already know it, as a matter of fact—that life moves in regions that extend beyond materialism, and that consciousness is not confined to the sensory field.

We have developed a general fear of the power inherent in the solar plexus. This fear has due warrants, for the solar plexus is unquestionably an important center of vital force. But in the East the solar plexus is recognized for what it is, and in Eastern psychic practices its potencies are understood and used. In *The Secret of the Golden Flower*,* Richard Wilhelm reproduced some drawings illustrative of Eastern meditation postures and processes, and in one of these the energies used in such techniques are indicated as originating in and rising from the region of the navel.

I do not mean to overstress these Eastern modes or mental attitudes, but I mention them in passing to indicate that Western psychism, including many of the practices of the Western mystics, is not a unique or new or strange psychological illusion, but has its natural roots and relationships far back in the earliest reaches of historical time. One who has had some experience in the psychic field is often led to wonder if the time has not come for the West to take into serious consideration those phases of human consciousness which, for the most part, we have allowed to lie dormant. In these present days one hears many expressions of aspiration toward a bet-

---

* In Richard Wilhelm (1938). *The Secret of the Golden Flower*. New York: Kegan Paul, Trench, Trubner.

ter human world. Such a development, if it is to be positive, will require a general and basic expansion of consciousness, a very positive widening of our fields of sympathy, understanding, and unprejudicial activity. And what is involved in all this is a necessary tempering of our materialistic code of values, the recognition and acceptance of other life-standards that are as immaterial as morals. After all, the key and base of all human projects is the individual psyche.

The individual psyche might be thought of as a facet of the universal, focused at its own particular angle and catching and reflecting the light of life in its own unique way. As long as it manifests in the physical world, it functions in a physical body. But the physical body is but an instrument for the use of the psyche, and behind all the substance and activity of the body the psyche *is* and operates. Out of the womb it comes with the body it is to use, and its use of that body depends upon the breath, from the beginning to the end of the cycle. All the colors and meanings of life that we perceive depend not upon the senses, but upon the psyche; and the color of life itself transcends our perception of it, as the atmosphere of the planet transcends our individual breathing.

Earlier in this chapter I have suggested that the temporary centering of consciousness in the solar plexus may be considered as a transfer of awareness from the conscious to the subconscious. But it should be emphasized that this is but a passing phase in a far more inclusive process. It is, in fact, an arc in a double circle composed of energy and awareness. The process originates in the control of the breath at the conscious level. With the proper manipulation of the breath, both awareness and energy become centered in the subconscious. But there ensues a subtle transfer of both energy and awareness into superconscious fields, for awareness is an expression of energy, and what consciousness experiences at this third level is achieved neither by means of the five senses nor by evocations out of one's personal past, for in many cases it is impossible that the particular experience should ever before have occurred in this world.

The superconscious experience itself may be thought of as the second arc of the circle of awareness and energy. There follows a third arc, in which both return to the usual field of measured time and space—the conscious. And here a fourth arc develops in remembering, analyzing, coordinating, and interpreting the experience. From a point within oneself one thus goes far afield and finally circles back to the starting point, bringing the fruits of the expedition with him.

What is outstandingly important in the whole adventure is the fact that one has temporarily been released from oneself. Consciousness is not confined, but free. Phase by phase, one has passed out of one's personality, so to say, and has made contacts in the field of pure consciousness, beyond the limits of egotism. I am convinced in my own mind that the soul is quite objective because, though it is undoubtedly a phase of the human consciousness, most of us never reach it—except perhaps in sleep and in the deepest need from within ourselves. The primary reason for this is that the soul partakes of the nature of the universal consciousness, while we rarely escape from the confines of our limited individualism. I believe that much of the color that I have described as appearing in supersensory activities I have come on by chance. Since it lies dormant and unsuspected, it is a phenomenon of imperfection and of relative inefficiency, and it occurs because the pure white light of true universality transcends the best that I have been able to accomplish in my psychic efforts to be wholly impersonal.

I am deeply convinced that, despite the analytical nature of these explanations, consciousness is one and indivisible in fact. Each one of us expresses as much of it as he cares to; and while we are undoubtedly delimited from ever expressing it all, we commonly fail to make even slight attempts to reach our own impersonal and supersensory levels. There the psyche, with its capacity for wide relationships, awaits the awakening of our consciousness, so harried by the physical, sensory, and civilized world.

That I have been successful in a measure is due to the fact that I am ready, by conviction and self-training, to give myself freely to life. Because of this fact I have accepted some of the disciplines which are the means to psychic development, and which—though in some ways different from those that lead to virtuosity at the piano—include desire, purpose, will, and concentration of attention—and possibly some good measure of supersensory attraction.

If I were to be asked what are the main features of special breathing in relation to supersensory activities, I would say that they consist in the achievement of a "realignment" of the various factors of the organism and a subtle shift in their internal relationships; that the operations of the metabolism are affected in consequence, and that one of the main effects of these alterations is a recentralization of consciousness. The breathing to which I have referred involves a withdrawal of awareness from sensory stimuli; and though the senses may severally continue to operate or not (one sometimes closes the eyes, for instance), awareness becomes concerned with stimuli that occur in a nonsensory field. I have an inner feeling of participating, in a very unified way, with what I observe—by which I mean that I have no sense of any subjective-objective dualism, no sense of I and any other, but a close association with, an immersion in, the phenomena. The "phenomena" are therefore not phenomenal while they are in process; it is only after the event that the conscious mind, seeking to understand the experience in its own analytical way, divides up the unity which, after all, is the nature of the super-sensory event.

Again, it is as though I became infused and active with a new flowing rhythm, a process which is very vital and very *interesting*, in the sense of being at once all-absorbing, all-revealing, and fulfilling. Precisely what is being absorbed, revealed, and fulfilled (in this deep inner sense) one does not know, for one is not looking on from an objective point of view, but is intimately participant *in* the process—yet the feeling of high competence, well-being, and creativity is of the essence of the experience.

I am quite sure in my conscious mind that these sensations of unity and fulfillment occur through some normal expansion of my consciousness; and since this happens through a predominantly *lifting* flow of energy from the solar plexus, and since it is accompanied by my awareness of such personal symbols as the bright spiral and the electric-blue pools that I refer to in the chapter on "Symbolism," I believe that the shift of consciousness which is the effect of the whole process occurs especially in the brain and in the glands in the head. I sometimes have a feeling of congestion in the forebrain and in the temples; sometimes there occurs a positive throbbing in the head. These effects disturb my supersensory concentration; and, becoming aware of them, I take them for signals that I am going too far out or am continuing the absorption for too long a time. They are metabolic warnings from the organism as a whole that the supernormal condition has been sustained for long enough, and that *it* will not be responsible for the effects of a further continuance of the dissociation.

It should be made very clear, however, that the breathing, the disso- ciation, and the "phenomena" of supersensory experience are not ends in themselves, even though each supersensory experience may be a thing by itself. The repetition of these activities has its inevitable natural effect in the subconscious, where all that happens to the consciousness becomes a part of the individual life-quality. And what seems to eventuate as these experi- ences accumulate is a universalization of one's life, one's point of view, one's attitude to people and events. There develops a generalization of response. By this I do not mean that one's perception of details is lost in any measure; on the contrary, the details of occurrences in the world become obvious and are quickly grasped. But one becomes accustomed to summing up a score of details into the larger significance that contains them all, and to perceiving the condition or project or problem in the terms of this larger meaning.

I am especially impressed by the realization that in the whole experience one loses many of one's ordinary fears. Out of the supersensory world one brings an inner *conviction* of the nature of universality, timelessness, and the continuity of being, and this deep inner "sense" becomes a key to the nature of one's criticism of life and one's judgment of events. It all amounts to a widened horizon in consciousness and a consequent extension of one's field of view, a field in which the data of physical and factual experience are seen as figures in a wider panorama of time and space, and are judged in the terms of an enhanced, impersonal, but sympathetic understanding.

Finally, as indicated in the first book of the Bible, it is through the purposive and powerful operation of consciousness that darkness and chaos are transmuted into light and into specific forms. The *process* of the change begins with the breath—the *word* says, Let there be light, and there is light. It emerges out of darkness, and it breaks into color and form for the serving and saving of man, once he learns to interpret the meanings of these. Subjectively or objectively perceived, colors and forms are all symbolic, and we grasp their significances as we are able. But the creative *power* in humanity is not perceptible to man's senses; it lies beyond manifestation, even beyond the human mind—where consciousness itself, in some measure synthesized, makes contact with the everlasting Universal.

VI
Healing

THE EARTH, THE WATERS, and the atmosphere of our planet are very ancient; and through the ages they have been the receivers of all the waste of the world. They are constantly active in the processes of repurification, transforming the decay of old life-forms into the reconditioned substances of new life. The substances of decay are the substances out of which new life is created at the physical level; and the soil, the waters, and the atmosphere—three of the basic factors on which all forms of physical life depend—are always more or less saturated with essences which are deleterious to physical life itself. Every exhalation of our breath tends to darken the atmosphere of our environment, and the ordinary wastes of all bodies are a menace to human existence.

This is the basic circle of all physical existence, and one of the mysteries of life—the synthesizing of diverse substances into new vitalized forms, the expression of life through these forms according to their respective capacities, the eventual withdrawal of vital forces from these forms, the deterioration of the physical synthesis into its elements, and the re-purification of these elements for use, again and again, in the construction of other synthetic forms for the further expression of the life-force. No wonder life remains a mystery to the mind of man. Death supervenes upon life, and life emerges out of death. The whole process operates under natural laws; and we are not equal to the comprehension of these laws.

Consequently, the world is full of distresses for mankind. This field of distress is one in which humanity differs from every other category in nature, because, by virtue of our innate capacities, we are creators of the means and manners by which life is expressed at the human level; and since we do create, we bring into being conditions that are both useful and adverse to our own existence.

The two common factors which give rise to the problems of healing are: the elements which are destructive of human well-being, and which exist in each of the four kingdoms of nature; and the ignorance which so often robs our creative power of its constructive values.

And here let me say that, as I see it, healing is not only—or even primarily—concerned with the physical diseases and disabilities that our human nature suffers from. The tap root of human difficulties reaches far below the physical level of our lives, and the manner in which we use our physical equipment is always conditioned by the deeper qualities and purposes of our psychological selves.

I have often been asked how much I know of medicine. I know nothing of medicine or anatomy or psychology, in the technical sense. Yet I am able to heal. When I do so, I am but the agent of a norm which comes to dissipate an abnormality; under any and all circumstances there must exist, within the psyche of the distressed individual, a fertile seed of the "will to live."

This will to live—which I am using here as a symbolic phrase—is fundamentally a psychological rather than a physical factor. Though in some cases recuperative power may seem to reside at the levels of physical activity, as in the healing of wounded flesh and the knitting of broken bones, nevertheless, in all conditions of disease and disability, including these, the will to live must exist (however unconsciously) as a basic fact in the individual psychology. And I would go so far as to say that successful healing consists very simply in the establishment of a regimen which releases this will to live from whatever conditions are inconsistent with and abnormal to it, and which may dominate it at any given time.

We make a grave mistake if and when we think that "healing" is principally concerned with the correction and cure of physical disabilities. Our physical equipment is in the nature of an instrument for the expression of our inner motivations and purposes; and our psychological qualities, rising constantly to the need for expression, motivate and determine our physical activities.

Does this psychological field seem vague or remote to our understanding? It is the field which, like a landscape emerging into visibility with the dawn, is becoming the object of attention for the consciousness of mankind. It is not by chance that psychology has broken away from philosophy and become an experimental science with a field of its own. Psychiatry is already proving its thesis of the sub-physical sources of abnormality and maladjustment in human life. We are experiencing the early stages of a new expansion of the racial consciousness—an expansion which is to be at least as important and definitive as that other expansion which changed man from a nomad into an agriculturist.

It is as though, having conquered four of the ancient elements of earth, water, fire, air, and ether, we are now proceeding to fresh experience in the field of the least substantial of them all, and to the discovery of the non-physical roots of our own existence. For in this new scientific advance man is turning the searchlight of awareness upon his own inner activities, and is discovering the immaterial energies that motivate his physical operations.

What the future effects of these new techniques may be are now unpredictable. To me it all seems to be an advance of human centralizations from the physical-emotional field into the areas of rational mind. Humanity is suffering so desperately (and so predominantly at the physical-emotional level) in the present world war, it seems inescapable that we shall learn something positive and definite from the race-agony. If we do, it must be in the nature of a conscious realization of what causes these wars and world-distresses. What does cause them is our failure to recognize, appreciate, and accept the fundamental laws of our human nature. Through its ignorance, its present lack of development, humanity creates its own malaise. But the healing of the nations, like the healing of individuals, is approaching—is entering into—a new area of psychological rationalism.

Fundamentally, there is but one kind of healing. Of course I do not mean to deny the inestimable values of medicine, chemistry, and surgery. But the physical areas, in which these techniques are for the most part helpful to human life, are based in the individual psyche. It is to this subtle factor in man that all healing, of whatever kind, is foundationally and finally related. To heal means to assist in the recovery of a condition of health according to the norm, whether this recovery involves a release from physical incapacity, emotional imbalance, mental delusion, or an arrest of psychic development.

But what constitutes the norm? That is what we do not yet know. Most human distresses may be said to be due to this lack of a conception of the norm. Our current investigation of psychological abnormalities is giving us some clues, however, while medicine and dietetics have found means, in recent years, for tremendously improving the physical condition of men and women—even having extended the span of life-expectation. But our future programs of true development lie in *fresh* fields of discovery, knowledge, and understanding; and we are opening up the vast continent of our own psychology because it is in that area that the norm lies hidden.

Humanity creates its own norms, its own concepts of well-being, development, and fulfillment. And it is obvious that these concepts are not modeled on the patterns of our physical environment, for the life of man transcends its environment and holds in solution all the qualities and talents of the universe. We have to learn how to use the power we possess.

Healing is achieved through comprehension—not only the comprehension of a particular given distress, but also the comprehension of that perfection of which the distress is a broken symbol. There must also be developed a comprehension of how and when the original perfection began to deteriorate into this. These factors are all to be discovered in the terms and at the level of the individual in distress; for in the last analysis, his own body and his own psyche must do their own healing, must achieve recovery according to their own conception of "perfection." In physical disability the healer can give assurance and symbols of health; in psychological distresses he can give assurance and symbols of integration; but of these only those will be helpfully effective which the deep consciousness of the distressed person can accept.

In experimental hypnosis it has been learned that in every individual there exists an egoic core which will resist suggestions that are incompatible with its own nature, no matter how amenable to hypnosis the person may be. In the recorded healings performed by Jesus, the psychological state of the patient was always the key—"Thy faith hath made thee whole."

Within each individual there resides the perfect form. To build a life adequately on that insubstantial pattern, the individual must become sensitive to the subtle pressures of necessity that arise within his own nature. Like the pitcher that comes into material being in accordance with an immaterial model of intention, purpose, and usefulness, the individual human life must be molded in the terms of an efficiency which is natural to itself. This inner pattern is an individualized fragment of universal nature; and the life which is erected on this foundation is meant to—and must, as far as it goes—conform to the qualities of the Infinite.

When such conformity with the Universal is achieved by the individual in a large measure, the life becomes a coherent pattern of relationships well defined and understood, and thus duties and responsibilities become living sources of activity filled with joy.

When anyone comes to me for help or healing I rarely listen to the story of the case. Instead, I see the condition as it is reflected in his *"surround."* A person's *surround* encloses and accompanies him like a misty aura, changing in color and density as his moods and conditions change; and it is in my perception of a person's *surround* that I find the clues to his inner state and conditions. Were I to listen to his story, I should be diverted from my own clear apprehension of his difficulty and his need. But seeing and feeling the brightness or the shadowed grayness of their *surrounds*, I sense the physical and psychological conditions of people—and not only of people, but of denizens of the plant and animal worlds as well.

To me, the only strange aspect of this capacity of perception is the fact that it is not common. That we do not penetrate beyond the obvious physical marks of fever, depression, pain, worry, and fear seems to me to involve a peculiar limitation of perception. Many people, without seeing any *surround*, develop this capacity of penetration in some measure, as the physician gathers an inner understanding of a "case" from the temperature of the body, the absence of vital force, stertorous breathing, or the dullness of the eyes. The expert in any line of activity is one who has learned to summarize his perception of all the symptoms or indications of a condition at a glance, and who comes very close, by "intuition," to the same sensing of a subtle state of being as I gather from the perception of the *surround*. In many cases, both for the expert and for me, it would be better if the person did not talk at all; but I have learned to leave people's words to the attention of my subconscious, while I gather my own clear understanding of their condition and their need by my own modes of perception.

In any case, the person's story, with all its positive and negative details, rarely amounts to a clear and concise statement of facts, though it does reveal the clues to the psychological state of the person. Such of these as coincide and fuse with other pertinent data which I "sense" will be contributed by my subconscious to the sum total of my perception. But very often the *key* to the problem is the one point which is missing from the person's own realization of the nature of his difficulty.

My understanding presently becomes clarified and simplified. This does not mean, however, that the process of "cure" will be simple also. The chemistry of psychology is not like the chemistry of the physical body; the emetic which will cause a person to eject a poison from his psychological system is often more subtle than any emetic known to medicine. I have often surprised and sometimes disappointed people who have asked me for help, by cutting them off in the middle of their story. This has had the effect of slight shock; it also has the effect of dissociating them from their condition and diverting their attention to me—frequently in resentment. There are many cases in which help can best be given, or can only be given, through an abrupt disruption of the psychological status quo. But where resentment is already the seed of the condition—as in anger, hatred, jealousy, and spite—more resentment is not what is needed, of course, although a shattering of the destructive concentration may be primary.

In any case of physical disability I know that I am simply the agent who responds to a need, and I give of whatever I have in the circumstances. I become an aid to the sufferer's "will to live." In fact it is the sufferer's will to live which seeks additional strength to save itself.

In all kinds of cases, the key to correction is to get at the root of the difficulty. Actually, perhaps, I am not interested in the slightest measure in the details of a man's life; but it is essential that he shall himself be interested in them in a certain way—a specific way: he must see clearly into himself and find there the deep relations to his present dilemma. So I ask him, "When did you first feel this pain?" or "When were you first aware that things were changing in your circumstances?" To answer, he inhales a breath; that is a breath of memory; and soon or late, it will drift down to the area of his psychological being that is waiting for its revitalizing effects. It may take time to do its work, but in any case the corrective regimen has begun.

There are many cases of distress which are purely psychological in their nature, having nothing to do with a person's physical condition as such, yet affecting the whole of the individual life. In such cases a measure of hypnosis, a play of illusion, "magic," is often the proper technique. Cases of inferiority, financial inefficiency, destructive bad habits, social maladjustments, and so on, are commonly based in some delusional attitude. The question then is, what different attitude, once induced, will let in the corrective light?

Though there are many therapies, there is but one kind of healing. Whether one "treats" a man in his physical organism or in his psychological states, one aims at the reintegration of the forces of his life. A person in an adverse psychological condition must get at the core of his difficulty through an understanding of its beginnings and through faith in his own ability to help in his cure. He often does this by some sort of objective "transfer," by fastening his attention on some object outside himself. In many cases, the first requirement is just such an anchor of faith in someone else; and when anyone comes to me in the hope or faith that I may be such an anchor, I always justify him by accepting, for the moment, the anchor role.

But such a person's attention must eventually be retransferred to himself. So one gives him the suggestion which will be self-corrective of his present state. Having thus centered his attention upon his problem, I often leave him to himself for a time, and let his own psychological metabolism do its work. Actually, I thus induce a measure of self-hypnosis in him. I have suggested a fresh concentration of energy and attention, have penetrated the confusion of a delusive attitude, and have given an anchorage to the man's faith—often an inestimable gift, as is proved by the miracles of Lourdes.

In some cases a greater measure of hypnosis is necessary than in others. This is achieved by further discussion, by the deeper concentration of the man's attention upon me as anchor, and upon the relationship between me and his difficulty. But actually, in all of this, his attention does not always have to be conscious; his subconscious will take it all in. And the subconscious will use it, moreover, in its own mysterious way.

We need to realize that in conditions of psychological confusion one's whole consciousness becomes like the atmosphere on a foggy day. Confusion, illusion, delusion—the fog has progressively thickened so that the man can no longer see out, can scarcely breathe. He suffers a state of actual psychological breathlessness. And this condition becomes so desperate—the fog crowds in so heavily—that the man is at last incapable of clearing his own immediate atmosphere. If a psychic breeze would only blow, he would be released from his deepest distress. So I raise a breeze for him, enable him to clear his own atmosphere, and presently he is able to breathe and to discern the light again.

Nobody asks for help in self-healing except when the will to live is still fertile within him. In such cases the body knows its own need, and the psyche knows its own need also. And having resorted to the search for help, both the body and the psyche—the consciousness as a whole—will accept such help when they find it. To be a conscious healer is to be always ready to give help, to the best of one's ability, and to be always sensitive to the subtle perception of humanity's various needs.

There are many unconscious healers—just as there are many people who unconsciously carry and diffuse both physical and psychological disease, debility, and despair. The ancient challenge, "Physician, heal thyself!" constitutes the first problem of the conscious healer; and the double duty of the conscious healer is, (1) to eliminate the elements of his own injuriousness in the world, and (2) to increase his power and capacity to heal on all the levels of life.

There are certain types of human distress, usually rooted in the emotions and the mind, but affecting the physical body also, in which one who can must do more than clear the psychological atmosphere in the ways I have already suggested. The whole field of the life, both natural and cultural, having been tilled to normal and creative consummations, is abruptly shattered by honorable outer forces, and one finds oneself ground and suffering between the irresistible millstones of the gods. There are many people—especially women—who are enduring this type of difficulty today. Having built their lives honestly, in conditions of peace and freedom, they find all the normal meanings of their lives swept away by the conditions of the war. They are patriotic, and they accept the necessities and sacrifices in principle, but are unable to make swift and easy adjustment to the changed order of things that is sweeping the world. They are not stupid people—rather they are generally simple and pure in their private purposes. Life has suddenly become too much for them; and like the protagonist in Greek drama, they move as they must along the paths of an overpowering fate. And these are paths of bitterness.

One of these women came to me, dry-eyed, but stretched to the breaking point. Her inner tension was apparent in her face and in her person; her nervous system was in riot, and in controlling it, she had become rigid, taut. She was sure that her husband, who was with the naval forces of the United States, had been killed. She knew that his ship had been sent into the southwest Pacific, and all the world knew of the hazards of those seas.

The death of her husband—an inevitably tragic event for her—would be the last phase of her descent into the abyss of despair, possibly of madness; and she was rushing forward into that phase as though fascinated by the idea of her own destruction. Yet she had had no notification of her husband's death, either officially or otherwise; her condition was wholly self-created.

What "treatment" could one possibly offer a person so spent and desperate? It was no time for platitudinous comforting; one could give no reassurances from one's own knowledge; the pressing need precluded all slow processes of recovery; but something positive was needed at once.

So, as I frequently do, I let her pour out her entire story. And then, with a gesture—as if I held the whole condition in my hands like a physical object—I placed it beside me on my desk. "There," I said, "I shall deal with your problem in my dream tonight."

The woman went away. And that night, in my telepathic dream, her husband came and talked with me. He assured me that he was not dead. He told me where he and his ship were. He mentioned by name people and places I had never heard of, and circumstances which were alien to my knowledge. These were references to South America, to deep waters, and to Ruby as a proper name ...

When I reported the whole experience to his wife, on the following day, she understood perfectly what he had meant in these references. And at the receipt of his message she recovered herself almost miraculously, realizing at once how she had permitted her imagination to undermine her fortitude. That was the beginning of her self-rehabilitation. She has entered into her new cycle of strength; she has achieved a new faith—it is as though she places her trust in her husband's existence and destiny because of a new understanding; and up to the present moment, that trust has been justified. Through him she is also beginning to realize the nature and meaning of the war and of her country's part in it. In fact, she is becoming individualized.

What type of person makes the best healer? Looking at the matter in the broadest terms, the extrovert, the man of action, is potentially the best healer. He breathes deeply; his blood flow is a strong current; vital energy moves in him freely; he generates a tremendous magnetism. Though he serves many idols, he is also a breaker of crystallized attitudes. He is powerfully active at the more obvious levels; and if you can induce in him—if he can induce in himself—a sympathy so potent that it will modify his activity and encourage him to give himself to the cause of healing, you have a strong new agency enlisted on the side of human welfare.

Yet it may be said that, as a matter of fact, the more contemplative introvert is more commonly the healer. He has a more just and sympathetic understanding of causes and effects, a keener sense of other people. He has the temperament. He canvasses the field of his work subjectively, rather than through outer experimental activity. What he lacks in force, compared to the extrovert, he makes up in the quality and readiness of his service. He has some good measure of psychological awareness which, above all, is the great essential dividing line between undiscriminated activity and creative action.

The objective for all of us—here as elsewhere—is to become what we are. Under some circumstances we have all had evidence of our healing capacity; somewhere, at some time, we have all eased somebody's distress; so we know that the power is in us. What we have to do, if we wish to heal the adverse conditions of human existence, is to cultivate our own inner quality by expanding the field of circumstances in which it can operate. This is primarily a matter of realization, achieved through conscious consideration and self-analysis. It really amounts to an enhancement of our own vital being.

Generally speaking, the extrovert needs to cultivate a more objective attitude, paradoxical as this may seem, for his activities are the effects of his strong inner impulsions, and being strong, he does pretty much as he likes. He needs to learn to pause and think twice before acting, to take habitually a second look to verify his first passing impressions. He needs to learn to understand before the fact, and to perceive independently of his senses.

The true introvert, on the contrary, has to learn to consider less rather than more, to come to his conclusions more directly and swiftly, more impressionistically, with less heavy-footed circumlocution. He also needs to amplify his vital force, generally speaking, and to be more adventurous in risking his conclusions and his good intentions in the fields of criticism and activity.

At this point I should like to insert another word about the breath. Whatever theories we may hold concerning either the spiritual or the physical genesis of life itself, we must all agree that the breath is the primary key to human life on this earth. Men can survive for some time without food, drink, or sunlight—the other main essentials to physical existence; but, as I have said before, to cut off their breath is to rob them of life at once. In the breath we have a mighty instrument for the development of the forces of living, and most of us do not sufficiently appreciate it or understand how to use it.

We are all familiar with the fact that our breathing is affected by the outer events of our lives—fear and shock and the excitements of contest—while the rhythms of laughter and tears, symbolized in the comic and tragic masks of the theatre, are respectively marked by the stimulation and the depression of our breathing.

In the conscious use of the breath, we have a tremendously effective technique for the development of creative capacities. I suppose the best known indicators of the effects attainable through conscious breath control are the various yogas of the East. Processes of breath control necessarily originate in the consciousness; and this means that, in the beginning, the breather deliberately projects awareness into the subconscious and undertakes to impose new rhythms upon that region of automatisms.

There is danger in this intrusion of the conscious upon the subconscious, for in such an undertaking one assumes direct responsibility for the management of the deep physical processes of his life—responsibilities which are commonly left to nature. No such practice should be undertaken except under competent direction and supervision. But when the control of the breath is achieved through the practice of correct regimens, a new unity is developed between the subconscious past and the conscious present. This unity can be achieved only through the practice of disciplines. Such disciplines have an objective which, of necessity, can exist only in the future. It thus becomes clear that the superconscious also enters into the unification of the consciousness, and that this new unity is qualified and dominated by superconscious determinants. The whole process lies in the supersensory field. Successful activity based in this new unity of consciousness depends upon a recentering of consciousness itself; sensory perceptions are inhibited or specifically intensified, as the case may require. To the best of one's ability, one induces or negates sensory effect, according to the specific aim and purpose of the concentration.

In my own work in telepathy, clairvoyance, and trance, the control of the breath is a primary factor. The precise manipulation of it always depends upon my present supersensory purpose. I refer more specifically to these processes elsewhere in this book. What I wish to emphasize here is that when the consciousness becomes unified and creatively active in a relatively high degree, much of the automatism of our habitual and routine living is transcended, and we consciously transpose the forces of life and of nature to new particular ends.

By the unification of the consciousness we also achieve a new relation to time. One finds each present moment related to the future rather than to the past, to the fields of burgeoning, fresh vitality rather than to the fields of obsolescence. Precedent rises into awareness when it is necessary to the criticism of oneself or one's projects; but on the whole, one progressively escapes from the drag of history, with its cynicism, ineptitude, and conflict, and goes free in the areas of clear aspiration. Basically, time and consciousness are respectively indivisible. To unify consciousness within itself is also to condition it to apprehend the unity of time. This is a key to the mystery of supersensory activity. Consciousness is capable of perception in fields that lie beyond the reach of the five senses. But the development of perception in these supersensory fields depends upon the development, by consciousness, of its own self-control. By the proper use of the breath we vitalize consciousness as well as the physical organism.

I trust I do not need to emphasize here the moral aspects of such activities. The whole field is fundamentally moral. One becomes responsible for one's activities—and their consequences—in an imperative sense. But one also learns, savingly, as one proceeds, that the law of compensation is inescapable.

The techniques and therapies of healing are numberless—chemistry, the readjustment of physical malformations, surgery, spiritual healing, the laying on of hands, prayer, meditation, hypnosis, psychoanalysis, electricity, diet, magnetism … Yet most of our cures are of the simplest kinds. It is not without natural warrant that the mother kisses her child's scratched hand or bruised knee. He comes to her in tears, and goes away laughing. Yet the mother is just a human being—sometimes a very ignorant one. But having love, she is always ready for service, and when the need arises she gives what she has—herself. Usually she contributes some kind of direct attention and a soothing bit of admonition and advice; but love is always included in her ministrations, and there is no one who can adequately fill her place.

This, I suppose, indicates the foundation on which all healing is based. One must love enough to be pure, in the sense of being quite selfless, and ready for service. The magic which is effective in the laying on of hands, or in any other type of helpfulness, must reach down to the subtle will to live that lies at the very heart of the individual existence; and it, being undeceivable, must gather the positive reassurance that it is fully related to the vitality of life itself.

There is only one kind of healing—the reassurance of the vital center within the physical form—the will to live. All states of being through which life expresses itself are therefore liable to the need of healing. A ready ear, a light in one's eyes, the sympathetic pressure of a hand, an encouraging word—any of these is often better "medicine" than all the drugs in the pharmacopœia. Fortunately, we are now entering into the field of human relationships in which these subtle psychological values are beginning to be really understood.

There is a certain sense in which nearly all of us are "patients" of one type or another, and subject to present healing. None of us attains to our full norm. Some of us live at a high measure of conscious efficiency and are constructive agents in the world. Such a full phase of conscious living often constitutes an excellent condition for continuous progressive development. But there are also conditions of almost utter unconsciousness in which not only healing, but even salvation occurs. Miraculous cures, which actually do happen, are of this type. Under some pressure of circumstances or dire need in one's life, one surrenders completely to the Universal—which is to say that one unites oneself wholly with the perfectly adjusted balance of natural forces in the universe; and partaking of that perfection, one is renewed in body, mind, and spirit. All healing requires some measure of this transcendence of our established individual habits and attitudes. On account of this, life frequently inhibits our usual activities quite completely, and puts the body to bed so that the individual's inner universalistic pattern may work its way undisturbed.

It is because of this same inner necessity that, always in time of war, miraculous appearances occur on the battlefield, and men are saved, against all odds, in the most desperate situations. One reads every day, in the newspapers, of events which transcend all known laws and all the probabilities of life, and indicate that when a man is reduced to the last outer extremes of physical and psychological endurance, he finds there an unrealized increment of being, in which each individual life is further related to life as a whole.

The hero in action, completely concentrated in his heroic activity, comes through a chaos of destructive fury unscathed; those very near death are delivered through the intervention of apparitions; men who have abandoned everything but faith live for weeks in open life rafts, without food or water; millions voluntarily suffer and die for causes that are completely impersonal to them …

In the face of such mysteries, and in the face of the ineptitudes of conscious human thought and planning, is it too much to suggest that humanity as a whole needs healing, and that the way to that healing is not to be found in the directions of ordinary sensory perception and "common sense"?

Illness or maladjustment, of whatever type, represents a conflict existing between the psyche and its environment. Healing consists in the readjustment of conditions in conformity to the needs of the psyche—the inner will to live. It is not always the individual that requires healing, however; very often it is the environment that needs readjustment. Consider the conquest of yellow fever or the present battles against syphilis and cancer; these involve not only the cure of individual cases, but the preventive elimination of environmental factors which are inimical to human life itself. And in the current war we have, on the largest possible scale, the battle of mankind against a threat of physical and spiritual conditions which, if established, would be intolerable to the hyman psyche.

Healing is concerned with the establishment and maintenance of a balance, a norm of relations between fragmentary and partial phases of the one Life. As a whole, this balance is established and inviolable. The battle which mankind is constantly waging againsts its enemies—including many factors in human life itself—is neither more nor less than humanity's effort (partially rational, but mainly irrational still) to discover and conform to its own norm of relations with the Universal.

VII
Death and Survival

THE WHOLE WORLD is familiar with death. Generation by generation, down the ages, all created forms have suffered disintegration and disappearance from the earth. And yet, in the inmost recesses of the nature of man, there has persisted a conviction that the death of the physical body does not involve the annihilation of the human consciousness. In the cases of many people this idea of man's survival of death is a pious hope, learned from religion, rather than an inner conviction of the psyche, for all the great religions that have deeply affected human faith have taught the reality of this survival.

In the East, the cradle of humanity, the teaching blossomed into what may be called a complete metaphysical science of continuity, culminating in the doctrine of reincarnation. And recently, in the West, the psychical research societies have attempted to prove survival as a fact, by recording, investigating, and verifying, as far as possible, the facts and the nature of psychic events of various types, and especially by recording—always for analysis and criticism—the messages which have been given by various "controls," ostensible discarnate entities who have themselves survived mortal death. These messages have been most commonly communicated by the controls through various "sensitives"—living men and women who have the capacity of suspending their consciousness in trance, leaving their physical mechanism free to the entrance and use of a "control personality." Generally speaking, the mass of messages which the controls have given in this way purport to come from the known dead, including the controls themselves; but the controls have done a great deal of other work of clairvoyant and telepathic types. They are not always dependent on the trance of a sensitive, but can sometimes communicate in other ways—by automatic writing, for instance, through those who are trained in this type of work.

Aside from religious teachings, philosophical discussion, and the massed evidence of the psychical societies, I am myself convinced that the spirit of man survives the death of the physical body. The conviction is the result of my own experience with the living, the dying, and the dead. I know that throughout the universe there are countless forces constantly in action, that these forces have form, and that though for the most part they are not perceptible to the human senses, they are in operation at my right hand all the time. I know that in the ultimate nature of the universe there are no divi-

sions in time and space. Psychically I can move out into these areas of relative immateriality and timelessness, and can in some measure experience
the conditions of the fields of being whose nature differs radically—not from
the *nature* of the human consciousness, but from the limited mass of concepts that constitute the present phase in the evolution of the human mind.

Is the human consciousness evolving? One has only to take a long view
of history to be assured that it is. This evolution is built out of cumulative
experience. The reception of the effects and fruits of experience by the human consciousness has been an accelerating process. Already the mind of
man has found the means for enveloping the whole earth, has penetrated
into immense distances of time and space, and has discovered many of the
rhythmic laws on which nature's continuity depends. It has at last discovered ways to live and to move under the sea; it has lifted the inertia of substance into the skies and made it mobile there. As in the womb, the human
embryo recapitulates and sums up the ancient stages through which life has
made its way forward in the development of form and capacity, so now the
human consciousness recapitulates and sums up, in its expressive activities,
the whole of life's age-long past experience. The human spirit has conquered
the objective environment, the entire "incarnation" phase of being.

But does all this prove that the human consciousness survives physical
death? Not quite. It simply proves that there are no known limitations within which the human consciousness is confined; it proves that, by the concentration of his attention and his will in certain directions, man can achieve
the "impossible," for he has done so again and again, countless times and in
countless directions. It proves that he can identify himself with whatever
interests him, and that his way of progress lies always, and precisely, in this
process of the identification of his consciousness with the alien, the "impossible." He can make human life—human nature—whatever he chooses.

We stand today on a hair line of consciousness that separates and unites
individualism and universality. We thus pay tribute to a concept of duality
in human nature that no other species knows. And in a manner that the
nations have never before experienced, humanity as a whole is thrusting toward the unifying of this duality. What this means is that, for the first time
in human history, on a world-wide scale, the human consciousness glimpses
the racial unity as a "practical" proposition ...

I do not mean to discuss this present progressive thrust of the human
consciousness. It is too immediate, too intimately close, for anyone to be
able to say how much it may actually accomplish forthwith. The forces of
the past are tremendously strong in the human constitution, and these reactionary forces will not be easily overcome. But the present phase of the
contest—focused at the moment in the oppositions of the World War—is the
first skirmish of man's consciousness in grasping, accepting, and bringing
into fact and form, a realistic working conception of the unity of human life.

Mankind is a unique creation, a category whose nature is divine —divine in the obvious sense that, like no other species living on this earth, it is capable of creatively transforming itself and its environment, capable even of conceiving its own immortality, and capable of creativeness in this direction also.

It is said that within the human nature there exist both a will to live and a will to die. Does anyone doubt that, by the concentration of attention and energy, man can determine which of these tendencies shall become dominant?

To my sense, man's conception of immortality is an ever-present guarantee of man's immortality as a fact. It is not conceivable that this idea could have originated anywhere in his objective environment. It is an intuition arising out of man's own nature. There have always been those who have cultivated this seed of immortality, and the cultivation has resulted in the deep rooting of immortality itself, as a creative ingredient, in the human consciousness.

The individual human life is a synthesis, made up of many factors, most of which are subtle and immaterialistic. The human consciousness is consequently complex. And its complexity allies it with countless relational affinities in the universe beyond itself.

The *life* in the human organism is the synthesized sum of many essences, and master of the body; and the death of the body occurs normally—barring, here, accident and disease—through the expansion of the life-quality beyond the capacity of the body to hold and serve it.

More than once I have seen this human life-essence release itself from the physical body, so that, without it, the body was dead. In each case I knew —I was *aware*—that it was the *synthetic essence* that had withdrawn, leaving each cell in the corpus alive and active at its own level, but bereft of its universe, its god, shorn of the supreme creative power that had controlled its destiny.

Can anyone actually imagine *himself* thus shorn of his universalistic affinities, his universe? It is impossible. Even those who hold opinion in suspense because they do not know, nourish the idea of immortality with the sustaining hope, within themselves, that it may be true …

The first time I saw the vital synthetic essence leave the body was at the death of a cousin, in Ireland, when I was a little girl. She was sleeping, and my aunt left me with her, to watch, with instructions to call her if Ann waked or stirred. My aunt knew, though I did not, that her tubercular daughter was very near death.

Ann finally stirred, in a kind of spasm, then lay quiet again, so I did not call. And I became aware of a dim mist that was exuded from her body, weaving intricately within itself in a rhythm that was without agitation, tension, strain, or pressure. Fascinated, I watched the faint small cloud move off into space. Did it leave the room by way of the window? or by penetrating through the wall? I do not know. Yet it withdrew, into infinite space, weaving within itself, and in utter concentrated absorption I watched it, followed it, accompanied it, into nameless psychic distances, until I was roused from my absorption by the entrance of my aunt. She, finding that her daughter had died in her absence, berated and punished me for having failed to call her.

Looking back at the incident, I have realized that in my childish ignorance I actually did not know in any conscious way that my cousin had died. But in psychic perceptiveness—which was the level at which I most truly lived in those years—I had intimately attended at the vital event.

Later, when my two sons died within a few months of each other, I was again aware of the withdrawal of that essence which is the sum of the synthetic human individuation. The dim misty cloud spiraled out from those small bodies as I held them in my arms, and moved away; and with an intensity of desire that was made poignant by my emotional feeling of personal loss, I followed those dim vitalities out and out into endless distances, till the throbbing in my head broke in upon the focus of my concentration.

As a small child (as I have told elsewhere*) I had drowned my aunt's ducklings and had seen the cloud that marked their death move away from their bodies as they lay on the grass beside me. In that and other early episodes, I first came to know that death is not a destruction but a change of condition, and that there is a place, divorced from substance, where the life-essence that we speak of as "the soul" or "the spirit" has a destiny beyond matter.

Later in life I again attended at the death of a friend, a grown young man, a Chinese, who was interested in psychism and was mildly psychic himself. He knew the religious teaching of the East and the West, and he had a reasonable faith in survival, through his intellectual understanding. He had consciously prepared himself for death, as far as possible. And when the time came, at last, I perceived two small clouds emitted from his body—one from the right side of the torso, at the level of the spleen, the other from the top of his head. Like the faint mists that I had seen in other cases of death, these moved out into space, weaving within themselves an intricate pattern of vitality.

One may feel that these psychic perceptions of the passing of synthesized sentiencies from their forms carry very little conviction relative to the survival of the human spirit. But here, as elsewhere, *my* conviction lies in

---

* In Eileen J. Garrett (1939). *My Life as the Search for the Meaning of Mediumship.* New York: Oquaga Press.

that inner knowing which is the core of all psychic experience. The events which I have described were more than mere attendances at a series of similar episodes. In a certain sense, there was nothing objective about them. They occurred as events, and I participated *in* them intimately, aware of their nature and their meaning, *knowing* what they involved and implied, what they *were*.

It is out of these experiences of death itself—the crossing of the hair line division in our consciousness—that I *know*, for myself, that death is not an end. The forms in which life dividedly expresses itself to our consciousness are all together the symbols of one among countless phases of being which constitute life as a whole. And though, at dissolution, the factors of a synthesis may be variously dissipated, the essence and value of the *synthetic achievement* are not. Every synthesis amounts to more than the sum of its parts, and this mysterious increment, this "more," is the creative end and purpose of the whole synthetic process. As the acorn and the apple are synthesized potentials capable of becoming ingredient in higher forms of synthetic life and consciousness than the trees that bore them, so the synthetic "more" of each human life is capable of becoming ingredient in states of being that transcend purely materialistic process and manifestation. This is the *way* of evolution.

G. R. S. Mead was a well-known occultist. He had been Madame Blavatsky's secretary for several years, and he lived in strict accordance with the faith that was distributed in his many books. I knew him very well, in the friendliest way, and between him and my daughter there developed a beautiful relationship of intimacy and understanding. When he died, I saw him in the evening after his cremation. My daughter had bought a bunch of violets for him, but as he died on that same day, they were not presented to him. She had intended then to take them to the funeral service, but in her distress at his passing they had been forgotten. They were now in a bowl on a table, a very present reminder to us both of our loss.

At five o'clock in the evening my daughter had the impression of him hovering over the violets, and though she was accustomed to hearing about the living dead, she was very much upset by this impression of his presence. She said he was calling for me. I was very sure that if it were possible for him to do so, he would communicate some message of reassurance to the world, and possibly some further occult revelation, for we had talked of the possibility many times.

On the strength of my daughter's quite clear impression, therefore, I went into trance, and I was permitted to see the form of G. R. S. Mead. He was not aware that the circumstances of his life had changed. The figure was recognizably he, but it was all drawn together, the back bent far forward, the head drooped low, with the chin resting on the chest and the forehead almost touching the knees; the eyes were completely closed, and the arms, folded across the diaphragm, rested on the thighs. The unconsciousness into which he had entered before dying was not over. Like a person in a delirium, he was still calling for Babs. He was sleeping—not as a human being sleeps, but as an embryo sleeps—a being in process of development from one state of existence into another. It was a form in which vital energies were mysteriously working to some fresh fulfillment. Beside him there were two or three rather wonderful old men belonging to the church. All his life he had been seeking communication with the Gnostic fathers, and they had evidently been waiting to receive him.

I have endeavored to give clear indications of two different aspects of my experience with death and survival. Between the two phases there exists a chasm which our understanding does not bridge. In watching the life withdraw from the bodies of those who were close and dear to me, I had no sense of personality in the weaving essences that departed. So far as I could see, there was no *identity* in the faint bright mists. They were as impersonal as a cloud or a patch of sunlight. Yet each cloud that forms in the sky *is* individualized, is what it is by virtue of the operation of certain forces and conditions working together in time and space. And each of the departing mists of life, weaving as they withdrew into infinity, was also a thing by itself, with a past history and a destined future.

Yet when I saw G.R.S. Mead (as I have seen many others among the dead) he was not vague and formless, but recognizably himself as I had known him as a living form and person. His figure was not substantial in the sense in which flesh and blood are substantial, but his appearance was definite and definitely individualized. He was himself and no other.

How the relative formlessness of the life-force at death takes on such subsequent form we do not know, any more than we know how unsubstantial thought creates images within itself. Actually, of course, it is no greater mystery than the development of the human body out of its generating seed. In the latter case, however, we have been able scientifically to follow the whole process of development through its various stages, while our ability to do this in the former case still lies in the future.

In my earliest years no one realized that what they saw fit to call my "wild imaginings" were solidly true for me—*a world I had to live with,* in other words. I *knew* the swirl of the wind, and the Irish peasants claimed I must be related to the pigs, for they were the only creatures that could see the wind. But I really knew its texture—as one who handles a gauzy fabric may rightly claim that he has touched its substance and knows its nature. When I spoke of the struggles of trees for light, that became visible as a turmoil in the woods, and of the battle of the flowers to the death if some careless or unknowing hand placed them in positions of disharmony, people shook their heads somberly over my condition. My glowing, dancing world, which interlaced itself with another world that seemed to be its own reflection, was never taken seriously by those around me.

It was easy for me, later, to believe that I might become a capable sensitive, since I saw much that to others was unseen. And in my visions of the alleged dead there were people who came and went with apparent ease, walking in harmony with the living as though some intangible, tenuous bond held the two worlds together. It was later that I began to understand that man carries within him a comprehensive map of his real self and the vast network of his relationships—a map which, could he but see it, would make him king of vision, instead of being crippled in his understanding.

My next step forward—to the controls—was taken as I have described.* I was ready to believe the assurances of those who claimed to know, that the dead wanted to speak and that they should be enabled to do so. Later I came to know that I was not certain of these things *in my own mind,* and a conflict developed within me, in consequence.

Before I became a sensitive, I had given much time to reflection on the fact of immortality. I did this, not because I was unsure; it was induced, rather, by the mysterious manner in which men thought of the hereafter. In all my youth I had heard the different churches and congregations proclaim God and the Spirit on Sundays, and then act, throughout the rest of the week, as though these did not exist. I often talked with the Catholic priest, Father Ryan, about "visions." He never doubted that visions were possible, but before the visions could be accepted as true, the Church had to legitimize them, in which case the visionary became a saint. The good Father never showed any signs of belief in my own eventual sainthood, for he admonished me to pray for release from the temptations of the devil which made me see them.

For me, the visions were genuine, realistic, and true. The conflict that later developed in my consciousness was not concerned with the visioning itself, but with the significances of it and with the uses I was making of it. Was I establishing communication? and if so, was it the thing that ought to be done? So long as research was the issue, my questionings were appeased. Research for the purpose of establishing knowledge and understanding in the public mind was important. Convincing the individual was important,

---

* In Eileen J. Garrett (1939). *My Life as the Search for the Meaning of Mediumship.* New York: Oquaga Press.

but only if that conviction allied him to the ultimate findings of true objective research.

There were many facets to the problem. I realized that while I saw the apparently living dead, it was always I who made the overtures. I also noted that the tempo of their being had to be considerably slowed down to meet my tempo, which had to be considerably quickened in order to get response from them. Of their presence, then, either in reality or in a form of reflection that took on all the semblances of reality, I had no doubt. But it was obvious that they became relatively denatured in the lowering of their tempo—as though inhibited—when they entered the area in which exchanges between us took place. I came to believe that, at their best and in their own condition, the departed gave of themselves to humanity, in enlightenment and grace. If this were true, then continuing to ask of them, continuing to hold them in a kind of devotional bondage to do their work according to *our* needs and desires, seemed wrong. I came to the conclusion that the dead are entitled to their freedom and their peace.

There seemed always to be guidance, quick and definite, if we needed it—answers to prayer and many blessings arising out of interchange between the two worlds; but a large part of our demand amounted to no more than the seeking of a sign—doubting "unbelievers" in the very thing we sought. We were asking for grace on *our* terms, rather than accepting it at the wiser hands of those who possessed it more fully than we. There also entered my mind the possibility that out of my own symbolism I had myself unconsciously rendered some part of the supposed communication. If, by any chance, this were true, I had a lasting doubt that I should continue to carry on communication at the old level and tempo.

The whole matter finally summed itself up in the conviction that, among all of my psychic capacities, "communication" was the weakest. This is my present viewpoint. I may be mistaken. But this brief statement will explain why I gave up work which was considered good, useful, and highly evidential. I should also add that I found that, on the whole, people very easily took communication for granted. Or they used it as a means of escape from the responsibilities of living. Even, sometimes, it was a game—a device used for amusement. But I saw many people progressively hurting themselves by simply presenting their problems to the departed and following the suggestions they received in response. So I felt, finally, that "communication" was not the way for me. And if I could see farther than those who could not see, then I must determine my own problem—which was not their problem—according to my own light.

No one who has had a life-experience at all resembling my own could possibly doubt the continuity of consciousness and the survival of the human entity after death. But in my own opinion—and I am sure this is so—there are vast differences between the entities that survive in the hereafter, just as there are vast differences between the people who are living here and now. But I believe that, from our point of view, all of these individualistic differences may be divided into two broad classes—those who seek the means to communicate with humanity, and those who do not.

I am convinced that in the usual conditions of life beyond death the interest in our current human world is no more keen and intense than is our interest in the hereafter. If we stop for a moment to consider how little thought *we* give to that future condition that awaits us all, we shall realize that, generally speaking, the "dead" are probably not yearning back toward the conditions of this life with any very special intensity.

There are many people who carry in their hearts so deep an affection for some dead relative or friend that an assurance of the continuity of survival, and a consequent ability to "contact" the dead person, constitute a primary need of their lives. The files of the psychic research societies are full of records of the fulfillment of such needs. But if I am to express honestly the values which have accrued from my own experience in years of work as a sensitive, I must frankly say that most of the people who request the services of a medium for communication are not always of this deeply affectionate and attached type.

During my years of such service, I was many times assailed by the realization that the work I was doing was of little or no value or consequence to either the living or the dead. On the one hand, in many cases, the seeking of communication became a habitual and established practice. There developed, unconsciously, a psychological dependence upon the information communicated which tended to rob the inquirer of initiative and creativeness, so that his life was in danger of gradually sinking into a condition of relative lassitude and lack of personal energy. On the other hand, as one examined a great many of the communications which such persons received, it became clear that their substance was of the slightest—no more, usually, than the receiving person could have arrived at for himself if he had put his mind to it.

Such realizations as these caused me a confusion of mind at the time. Yet I continued with the work, because I was myself in very much the same state as these inquirers of the dead—depending upon the assurances of living persons, in whom I had confidence, that the work *was* of value and importance. Looking back over the years, I am of the opinion that the work *was* and still is of value and importance. It is necessary for each new development, of whatever kind, to establish itself in the common mind. Once adequately established in the general consciousness, it is then destined to be dealt with according to its deserts and according to the capacity of public opinion to receive it. Thus, through the early practice of Spiritism, we have come to a high measure of assurance of individual survival beyond death, and to the beginnings of scientific investigation of supersensory faculties.

I have a very real sympathy for the bereaved person whose devotion is so deep that assurance of the survival of a dead friend seems imperative if he is to accept the change which has occurred in his own life. I believe that such assurance should be given, and I shall help distressed people in this way whenever I can. But I am firmly of the opinion that when communication has been established, and when the assurance of it has been accepted, the whole event should be treated with gravity. Every communication should be held up to the light of reason, good sense, and caution. Each communication has to make its way through the freed consciousness of the sensitive and penetrate the curiosity, need, and expectancy of the receiver, and somewhere in the process it is possible for it to take on colors that are not strictly its own.

It seems to me obvious that the mind may sometimes draw upon the frame which has been established in the subconscious agency, and it is my opinion that each communication must be sifted for its verities and realities. Communication cannot be an easy process even under the best of circumstances. A judgment of its values should never be hasty. Patience and perseverance are necessary if results are to be of sound value.

At the same time, I deeply believe that there is a positive and practical need for these communications to be studied and understood. We need to discover the methods by which communication is established between the two states of being. I make a sincere plea to the scientists that they have patience with "the follies of psychic researchers." Many of them have no hesitation in condemning genuine psychic experiences, without even considering the possibilities of many legitimate claims that have been offered—offered sometimes even by their more sensitive brothers in science. To condemn the practice of communication wholesale is to condemn the very foundations on which all religious philosophy is founded—a most unscientific attitude. I earnestly ask that the scientific methods of inquiry and cautious declaration be exercised here as elsewhere.

Most of the dead are just as incapable of communicating with the living, as most living people are incapable of communicating with them. And while it is fairly simple for the sitter here to formulate a question concerning some matter or event that is of present interest to him, I think we go much too far in expecting the dead to meet the inquiry on a level of equal interest. We have no good warrant for supposing that the dead are always ready to respond to our beck and call; and if they are not always ready, can we blame them if they respond to our approaches in inconsequential terms?

A large part of the criticism of Spiritism has been due to the inconsequential and trite nature of much of the material which has been received in psychic work. To me, a great deal of such criticism seems valid; but it should not be used in an endeavor to cancel the reality of humanity's survival of death. It can be constructively used instead, to improve the general understanding of the actual relationship which exists between the living and the dead.

Stating the case at its simplest, I believe the dead should be allowed their peace. They have not died in order to continue to live as they have lived here. In death, they have surrendered up much of what we know as their personalities—physical body, senses, and sensations, and they now have an insubstantial kind of work to do. We do not know many of the facts of man's condition beyond death. It may very well be, as I believe, that the dead retain some sort of "etheric" or "subliminal" body for some time. If so, that body is both a fruit and a seed—the fruit of the individual past and the seed of the individual future. From the teaching which we have all received, most people are more or less ready to believe (however vaguely) that what survives is one's soul. Since so few people know what the word "soul" means, however, it may be indicated here, from ancient texts and without elaboration, that the human soul is the psychic factor which exists between the Universal Spirit and the individual ego, and is a condition of fusion between the interactive qualities and experience of both the whole and the parts. By means of the soul the hosts of individuals remain united to the universal. The soul is the way of individual development and evolution. And since religion, in its spiritual aspects, represents a natural process in which the individual "binds itself back to its source," the soul is the path by which this return to the primal spiritual purity and unity is made.

Our education and experience in this world are predominantly colored by the qualities of substance and phenomena. Yet as time goes on and human nature continues to develop in areas of expanding freedom, it becomes more and more obvious that the outer substances and events which we experience are themselves the products of insubstantial energies and forces which, striving for expression, achieve activity in materialistic fields. But there is this to be observed: no human life is ever completely expressed, no human project is ever completed and finished. Down the ages, the fullest flowering achieved by one epoch has been the seed of another. This is because the human consciousness, partaking of the nature of life itself, is continuous and without end, and eternally expansive. To every manifestation of existence which consciousness encounters it reacts; and in this continuous give-and-take between the universal environment and the individual capacities for impression and expression, the individualized consciousness develops toward universalism. Our egotism is a fragment of a whole—the universe, the eternal Unity. Like that simplest form in the chemical content of all substances—the atom—we are each and all ingredient in the whole. We are thus inseparable from the universal, and the purpose of our experience in this world is the discovery of the mystery of substance and a realization of those insubstantial powers which all physical forms and activities manifest. The spiritual core of the individual is the indestructible spiritual atom.

In death we surrender substance—the substance of our own physical bodies and their relations in the substantial world. But consciousness does not disintegrate as all true atomic forms disintegrate sooner or later. Like the seed that becomes the forest tree, and endures the vicissitudes of development through a hundred cycles of shedding and renewing its foliage and fruit, the human consciousness, once individualized, is the seed of a process the destiny of which it is, through cycles which we do not understand, to become a creative factor in the evolutionary processes of the universal life.

There are phases of quiescence in this long process. We commonly think of death as such a quiescent phase. But just as we daily abandon the world in sleep, and so renew and revitalize all of our capacities for further living, it is probable that in death we fuse the diverse impressions of our earthly experience into a new and unified capacity for more abundant living.

As a child—possibly a too fanciful child—I knew and understood myself related to every living, breathing atom. I saw myself complete in the body, and I saw myself a mass of moving energies that could shape themselves into a thousand forms. Since I thus conceived myself in what many would be pleased to call the realms of fantasy, the impressions were absolutely my own, utterly real, and inescapably enlightening. I saw myself related to all the constellations, and to the whole of life. I perceived that true individuality does not consist in the aggressiveness of leadership, nor in the passivity of the one who would follow, but consists in complete agreement, without aggression, in the excellence (sometimes hidden) in the minds and hearts of the human majority. I learned the uses of self-negation, and how it becomes the true affirmation of life, and I thus understood both my rights and responsibilities as a part of all the world. And so my conviction of the indestructible self grew and developed until it was a basic truth, a factual reality. It is a part of all the tenuous inner knowledge that everyone has—instinctive and intuitional. It is my natural, non-rational sense of the All-knowing, in which *I* am a living part.

My decision to withdraw from the practice of communicating is in no sense a departure from my faith in survival. Of the survival of the spirit in man I am deeply convinced. Having added, here, my knowledge, born of experience, to humanity's dawning appreciation of its own worth and destiny, I shall not further amplify the theme. But in behalf of the human spirit, I add a stimulating word from the thought of a human mind of synthetic quality and greatness, the late Henri Bergson:[*]

---

[*] In Henri Bergson (1931). *Creative Evolution.* New York: Henry Holt & Co.

The great error of the doctrine of the spirit has been the idea that by isolating the spiritual life from all the rest, by suspending it in space as high as possible above the earth, they were placing it beyond attack, as if they were not thereby simply exposing it to be taken as an effect of mirage! Certainly they are right to listen to conscience when conscience affirms human freedom; but the intellect is there, which says that the cause determines its effect, that like conditions like, that all is repeated and that all is given. They are right to believe in the absolute reality of the person and in his independence toward matter; but science is there, which shows the interdependence of conscious life and cerebral activity. They are right to attribute to man a privileged place in nature, to hold that the distance is infinite between the animal and man; but the history of life is there, which makes us witness the genesis of species by gradual transformation, and seems thus to reintegrate man in animality. When a strong instinct assures the probability of personal survival, they are right not to close their ears to its voice; but if there exist "souls" capable of an independent life, whence do they come? Where, how, and why do they enter into this body which we see arise, quite naturally, from a mixed cell derived from the bodies of its two parents? All these questions will remain unanswered, a philosophy of intuition will be a negation of science, will be sooner or later swept away by science, if it does not resolve to see the life of the body just where it really is, on the road that leads to the life of the spirit. But it will then no longer have to do with definite living beings. Life as a whole, from the initial impulsion that thrust it into the world, will appear as a wave which rises, and which is opposed by the descending movement of matter. On the greater part of its surface, at different heights, the current is converted by matter into a vortex. At one point alone it passes freely, dragging with it the obstacle which will weigh on its progress but will not stop it. At this point is humanity; it is our privileged situation. On the other hand, this rising wave is consciousness, and, like all consciousness, it includes potentialities without number which interpenetrate it and to which consequently neither the category of unity nor that of multiplicity is appropriate, made as they both are for inert matter. The matter that it bears along with it, and in the interstices of which it inserts itself, alone can divide it into distinct individualities. On flows the current, running through human generations, subdividing itself into individuals. This subdivision was vaguely indicated in it, but could not have been made clear without matter. Thus souls are continually being created, which, nevertheless, in a certain sense pre-existed. They are nothing else than the little rills into which the great river of life divides itself, flowing through the body of humanity. The movement of the stream is distinct from the river bed, although it must adopt its winding course. Consciousness is distinct from the organism it animates, although it must undergo its vicissitudes. As the possible actions which a state of consciousness indicates are at every instant beginning to be carried out in the nervous centers, the brain underlies at every instant the motor indications of the state of consciousness; but the interdependency of consciousness and brain is limited to this; the destiny of consciousness is not bound up on that account with the destiny of cerebral matter. Finally consciousness is essentially free; it is freedom itself; but it cannot pass through matter without settling on it, without adapting itself to it; this adaptation is what we call intellectuality; and the intellect, turning itself back toward active, that is to say free, consciousness, naturally makes it enter into the conceptual forms into which it is accustomed to see matter fit. It will therefore always perceive freedom in the form of necessity; it will always neglect the part of novelty or of creation inherent in the free act; it will always substitute for action itself an imitation artificial, approximate, obtained by compounding the old with the old and the same with the same. Thus, to the eyes of a philosophy that attempts to reabsorb intellect in intuition, many difficulties vanish or become light. But such a doctrine does not only facilitate speculation; it gives us also more power to act and to live. For, with it, we feel ourselves no longer isolated in humanity, humanity no longer seems isolated in the nature that it dominates. As the smallest grain of dust is bound up with our entire solar system, drawn along with it in that undivided movement of descent which is materiality itself, so all organized beings, from the humblest to the highest, from the first origins of life to the time in which we are, and in all places as in all times, do but evidence a single impulsion, the inverse of the movement of matter, and in itself indivisible. All the living hold together, and all yield to the same tremendous push. The animal takes its stand on the plant, man bestrides animality, and the whole of humanity, in space and in time, is one immense army galloping beside and before and behind each of us in an overwhelming charge able to beat down every resistance and clear the most formidable obstacles, perhaps even death.

VIII
Symbolism

EACH OBJECT THAT IS SEEN in the world, each sound that is heard, each scent and taste and touch, is an expression of some state of being that is objective to the consciousness that is affected by it. For the most part, we take these things for granted; yet if we were consciously to penetrate into the life-history of the objects which furnish an ordinary room, for instance, we should become involved in an endless mass of data and find ourselves nonplused by the states of being that lie just beyond the familiar surfaces of objects that we see and use every day. Behind everything that we sense—from the aroma and flavor of our breakfast coffee to the last sound that reaches us before we go to sleep—there broaden away vast fields of significance of which, for the most part, we never become aware.

Generally speaking, our senses present to us only the surfaces of life; present moments in long sequences of cause and effect. The sensed moments are fragmentary symbols of long lines of life-in-process, and it is within the capacity of the human consciousness, not only to discover the factual data of these lines of vital force, but also to measure the relative values and significances which they symbolize.

What, then, is a symbol? It is a sign, in form or movement, representing states of being which stretch away from it in time and space; it is an ideogram, a hieroglyph, revealing hidden subtleties of being. The perfume is the symbol of the rose—its life and nature; the acorn is the symbol of the oak, which has itself become the symbol of life-qualities of strength, sturdiness, and endurance; the printed page is a symbol of the whole creative ingenuity of man, as well as the revealed image of a human individual at work weaving a romance or a learned treatise into form out of the unsubstantial areas of his knowledge, imagination, intuition, inspiration, and inner perception.

In the last analysis, all *natural* symbols represent the adventure of the immaterial life-force as it dawns and fades in and out of the categories of separate forms. And all man-made symbols are records of the adventure of the human consciousness in areas of discovery and self-expression. Every form is a signal and an appeal to man's sympathy and comprehension. All of our original understandings arise in our perception of the significances of natural symbols; and we all know from our studies in chemistry, the law, business, and art, that the appreciation of cultural symbols involves the penetration of consciousness into the depths of their meaning.

It is the nature of the human mind to perceive by way of the media of images. Form may be said to be the field in which the faculties of perception operate; but perception is not understanding. The *meanings* of the life of the world, as it appears to each perceiver, depend upon the values which his subtle mind is able to read into and read out of the forms perceived. In each and every case, such interpretations depend upon the innate life-quality of the interpreter, natural and acquired, and consequently, the world we all live in is what each one of us makes it for himself.

If we turn from the sensory field to the field of supersensory perception, we find that here also the apprehension of reality occurs through the medium of symbolic images. The significances of many of these impressionistic symbols have been rationalized by both religion and science. It is almost impossible for us to understand how a civilization could have managed its mathematical affairs by use of the Roman numerals only, without the Arabic figures and the decimal point; while on the other hand a whole philosophy of significance has grown up around the Christian symbol of the Cross.

What may amaze one who comes freshly to the perception of the non-sensory imagery of the mind is the fact that it is a synthetic product, consisting vaguely of images from the world that one knows from sensory experience, with something added. Yet both the perception and the interpretation of super-sensory symbols are bound to be purely personal reactions. And the crux or key to the individual's expression of what is perceived lies in an intuitive "click" of psychological understanding by which the perceiver *knows*—and knows that he knows. It must not be imagined that this "click" occurs through the operation of some magic trick. It is in truth magical, since we do not understand how it works; yet it is no more magical than our recognition, through sensory perception, of a particular distant star. It simply does occur, as a psychological event, in the natural relations of things.

In the human mind there is a continual creative energy interacting with our will. Its shapes appear, its sounds vibrate, and we describe these manifestations as symbols revealing the Absolute or the Universal to the individualized self. It is not difficult to understand that most people relegate the language of symbols to mystical and religious walks of life, forgetting that we can communicate our most common thoughts to one another only by means of symbols. I believe that each one of us possesses his own inner sign or symbol language which, however, has been lost sight of as we have become absorbed in the learned response. Form is necessary to life if we are to experience any sensation. Abstract mind itself contains no form, as those who meditate deeply know; but there are a light and a radiance that are always supersensibly available to consciousness. Out of this inner radiance light lines stem which, in turn, seemingly interlace and separate into forms;

and these, for want of a better word, we again describe as "abstract." Form being necessary to the experiencing of meaning, it dissociates (and unites) the parts and the whole.

The church has used symbols to preserve and teach its creed, and it has identified its laws and sacraments with symbols, to preserve their spiritual significances. But I am not here concerned with those symbols that have been accepted by scholars or repeatedly revealed by the mystics, but only with those that have been gathered through the operations of my own mind.

For me, all symbolic forms are naturally united with color. All of *my* forms are related to color. The white, gold, opaque, and pearly shades signify calmness, peace, tranquility. The red shades connote vigor and strength. The deep maroons and purples express growth and purpose that stem from the life of the individual being in struggle, suffering, and achievement. I am never conscious of black; purple in its darker shades seems to fill its place—I might almost say that in the vitality of life itself there is no black, no negation or emptiness such as black might intimate. Green is the coloring of all growth, and is symbolic in itself of the strength to develop and expand ...

When I say that symbolism is related to color, I mean that the symbols actually present themselves in color as they gather strength beyond their very first appearance out of the light lines. Nearly all of the symbols that I am familiar with are symbols of growth, development, expansion, and most of them appear in the cool green setting.

All subjective movement, such as that of which I am speaking, is born out of light radiance into lines and then into form. These forms come into being spontaneously; but they become somewhat concretized as one becomes familiar with their significances. I have no doubt that everyone has this tenuous symbolic drama taking place behind his eyes; but it is contemplation that makes us aware of it.

I also have no doubt that my symbols are related to my nature—my thinking and feeling, my character and personality. They are rarely perceptible for more than the seconds it takes to be aware of them. Nearly all of them occur in lines of graceful, flowing movement. Plants and animals wave into being out of the light curves. Purple plants, clothed with green verdure, may suggest a dense jungle growth—and out of the jungle, waves of color clothe emblems and figures, the colors themselves having deep and vital values. Plants and animals of weird but beautiful design change and re-change from darkness into light, and disappear again. Nothing stands still, for the forms are products of subjective processes forever in creative movement.

I feel sure that each one of us builds his inner thought forms differently, though the basic symbols and forms are all undoubtedly related, since thought is universal. The archetypal imaging of life, forever changing and creating its forms anew, moves across the sky of our subjective vision, if we give time to contemplation. Contemplation, volitional or unconscious, is the state in which our subjective perception develops, and its constantly moving significances are eventually translated into action and expression, qualified by the nature and capacity of the perceiver.

The yew tree may be considered as my primary life-symbol, because it has been a constant companion of my consciousness since the days of my earliest recollection. I am quite sure in my own mind that it represents one of the most important products of my creative capacity; and while it has not been possible for me to discover in memory the point of its inception, I am sure that I have created it out of the capacity-substance of my consciousness as a whole.

The yew tree was a familiar form in the landscape of my first natural environment. In Ireland it is a common feature of all churchyard scenery. Rationalizing its symbolism at this moment, I can do no better than to suppose that it somehow bridged, for my general unhappiness, the gulf that separated my tense life from a spiritual peace which I could mystically remember or which I intuitively knew. In certain brands of psychological theory, this peace would be the pre-conscious peace of the womb. Lacking, as I did, the love and living presence of my mother, which are the principal means by which the consciousness of most children is acclimated to the phenomena of this world, I very probably turned to the yew tree, personalizing it with attributes which were essential to my living and which I did not find anywhere in the world of human beings around me.

Very closely associated with this vital need of my early childhood were "the children," those realistic young creatures with whom I played—lacking other young companionship. The children were idealistic (and ideal) playmates. And whatever their physical constitution—if any—may or may not have been, they were absolute *realities* in my life. I saw them and talked with them and knew them as individuals. I was able to accept them, to serve them, and to receive their reciprocal service. They were a source of freedom in my life and of expansion for my consciousness. Were they wholly the product of my imagination? Not wholly. For, granting for the moment that they had no substance of their own beyond what I gave them, nevertheless, behind the reality which they had *for me* there existed and moved both my psychological need of them and my psychological capacity to create them. Both this need and this capacity were the most deeply fundamental realities of my own existence. They were products of the very core of man's creative capacity.

To my sense, this area that lies between the imperative needs of the human psyche and the forms which those needs bring into existence in the world is the area in which psychology should be primarily interested. One has complete sympathy with the practice of psychotherapies in "abnormal" individual cases of maladjustment, psychoses, and so on; but to me it seems that the field of "normal" human activities is the place of true illumination. We have artificialized our sense of values into a high measure of inadequacy, not to say uselessness; and I personally resent it when, for instance, my own creation of "the children" out of the need of my life is called "abnormal," while a rich man's erection of a building that will "pay for itself" is considered a thoroughly "normal" undertaking. I am quite sure in my own mind which of these two activities is the more direct and natural expression of human nature. That we may not all see it with equal simplicity indicates the very point I mean to make.

To return to the yew tree. Like a goddess, I endowed it with attributes out of my own wish and will—attributes that had not been given to any yew tree by nature. Instead of leaving it dark and somber, though beautiful, I made it gay; and I released it from the immobility of its association with churchyard stillness and made it active, pliant almost to the point of fluidity. Thinking of my yew tree symbol, I have often realized the magical uplift with which the Christmas tree affects children. Imagination, hope, desire, mystery, anticipation, aspiration, faith—a hundred facets of psychic capacity play upon an idea, and lo! there it stands on Christmas morning, in full reality, a factual fulfillment for the psyche. The moment of the impact of this fulfillment upon the psyche is the fullest moment of one's living. Whatever disappointments or delights may result from the Christmas tree's actual measure of largess are keener—sweeter or more bitter—than any other possible experiences, except those to which we may give ourselves with an equal psychic creativeness—as in the confused surrenders of love.

My experience with the yew tree never went beyond the magical moment of impact. I expected nothing tangible from it, consequently it never disappointed me. Every moment of my experience with it was filled with surprise, fulfillment, and delight. It became a dancer (though I have no knowledge of having made it a dancer); it flowered—variously; it divided itself into several yew trees, and in this division the parts took on separate personalities. It was a companion, a friend, a spectacle, a surprise, a mystery, and a constant fulfillment; and if I was myself the producer of all this marvelous delight, like the child and the Christmas tree, I was not aware of the source of all the wonder. And when, at night, I wearied from the day's activities, the yew tree too became sympathetically quiet—gently and darkly still—and I slept beneath its friendly shape.

I have no doubt that I myself created the essence of the significance which the yew tree symbol has for me. If I did, it was one of the best pieces of creative work in my whole life. For it has never abandoned me—which means, of course, that it continues to be useful to my psyche. As in the beginning, so now, it is the symbol of a state of being into which I escape from whatever turmoils, pressures, or preoccupations bother me in the outer world, and find the place of my own inner, unified, creative being. I frequently use the yew tree symbol as a means of achieving my psychic centralization or focus. Most of us lose this capacity to return, by completely giving ourselves over to the sensory world; but as I have indicated elsewhere in this book, in our best creative states of consciousness we have to find that non-sensory center of unity within ourselves.

If you mention such an experience as the yew tree to the psychologists you are very apt to encounter the word "infantilism." But one must remember that this word is just another symbol—frequently a symbol of a lack of understanding; and that One has said that to become as a little child is the way to spiritual salvation. People are apt to think of this teaching of the One as a paradox of religion; but it is a psychological fact of the most practical kind. Without being mystical or religious, one may suggest that—as Jung has striven to make clear—salvation consists, *for everyone*, in the fulfillment of one's own psychic nature. Looking closely at any given life, one can tell in a moment whether the individual is saved or lost. And having done this many times, with many people, one is moved to emphasize the values of the inner non-sensory psyche, and to recommend the recovery of the hidden mementos of early unity which are to be found there.

As a person progresses in life, he usually specializes in some particular line of symbolism—the arts, mathematics, chemistry, or whatever. And he becomes what he is through the identification of his life, in greater or less measure, with the realistic significances which the symbols represent *for him*. Everyone develops within himself, either consciously or unconsciously, a temperamental tonal key of his maturity, so to say, with which all the events of his life must harmonize or be judged, by him, adverse. This basic tone of a man's life has its symbol; and if he can consciously discover that symbol within himself, he will find it a means for normal psychic release—a release and expansion of his whole life and consciousness.

In my own case, this mature symbol, originating later than the yew tree, and not displacing it but having different capacities and values, is the motile bright spiral.

I have sometimes thought of this self-evolving spiral as a tool, like an awl, with which I bore my way into the universal—though there is never any sense of labor in that process. As a thing in itself, it operates without my volition, though the whole activity in which it emerges as a phase is usually volitionally induced. The spiral seems to me to be a projection outward from the spot in the center of my forehead, between the eyebrows.

Behind the spiral's weaving of its bright circular projection, I am at the same time aware of two limpid blue pools within and behind my forehead. They seem larger than the spaces occupied by my eyes, and within them there is a constant quiet motion, as of gentle electric energies in circular activity. I have an inner sense of these moving blue pools as emotional and creative. Emotion is such an important factor in all human activity, it must necessarily be ingredient in supersensory preoccupations. But the emotion I am here referring to is not so much *feeling*, in the sense in which we usually understand that word, but rather an expectancy, an anticipation, such as one might experience in concentratedly watching for the first appearance of the sun at dawn. Yet this simile fails to do justice to the real poise of the consciousness in this condition, because there is no sense of waiting in time; one looks *beyond* the horizon and knows that the sun *is* rising, and realizes the process *as a whole*. It is in this poised state, that *knows* by means of a *subjective* extension of consciousness, that I do my clairvoyant work; for me, the bright spiral and the two pools of Christmas tree blue are the symbols of the clairvoyant capacity.

There is a third symbol which is common to my consciousness—the trefoil, a three-lobed form, like a clover leaf or a shamrock. Actually, this is a four-part figure, with the stem side open, and I am reminded by it of Jung's treatment of mandalas and his insistence upon the four-part nature of man's psychic completeness. Nevertheless, I myself usually think of it as a three-part form. When it appears, I know that I am then capable of healing. To my consciousness the figure is usually rose-colored, and I conceive it to be the symbol of my innate quality at its best. This "best" means that I am then free in the very fullest sense, completely released from personality affairs and feelings, inwardly ready and capable of useful objective service. To me, this rosy three-petaled figure—a true flower of the psyche—suggests the esoteric meaning of love, which is our common human emotion lifted into the field of unity, the field of depersonalized being.

The symbols to which I have specifically referred, and which I consider as having special significances for me, have been the products of different psychological states—products of progressive phases of my own psychic development. The yew tree was largely the product of my childhood fantasy; nevertheless, it was a creation of my insistent psychic life. The bright spiral, with its associated blue pools, is the product and the sign of my capacity to project my consciousness into that phase of *consciousness as a whole* which may be thought of as the great *unconscious*. In the psychic condition in which I am aware of the presence of the spiral and the blue pools, I am clairvoyantly capable and can perceive beyond time and space. And when I am aware of the four-part form (which I sense as a trefoil pattern), I know that I am capable of working at the highest excellence to which my entire nature has achieved—I am then at "my best."

These three symbols I think of as "mine." They are subjective signals corresponding to the green lights on our traffic routes, and they tell my consciousness to "go," each at its own specific level.

My yew tree symbol is as clear an indication as anyone could wish concerning the inner need of my life at the time of its origination in my consciousness. The reason why it has not been outgrown and long ago forgotten is that it was so deeply and intensely vitalized by the psychic forces of my life. But all of one's deepest psychic needs are intensive. To catch the symbol that marks one's clear experience of self-realization is a vitally important achievement of the consciousness, and, as in the case of my yew tree, by reviving the symbol one can always find the way back to those truly basic depths of one's self.

The three symbols of which I have been speaking may be thought of as subjective forms. They occur as different phases *within* my consciousness. Beyond them, in areas of objectivity that are directly opposite to the materialistic areas of the sensory world, I perceive, in telepathy, an array of other symbols that appear and disappear as moving, momentary impressions in waving strata of shape and color. Individually these objective symbols often have no specific meaning of their own—or rather, each one of them represents a part of a meaning, which presently develops and comes clear through the association together of several of them. It is in this perception of a *whole* item of significance, compounded of the swift successive appearance of diverse parts, that the mysterious "knowing" of the psychic lies. There is in this "knowing" an assurance, a certainty, that transcend equivocation and ambiguity, because there occurs in the consciousness of the psychic a mysterious swift understanding, a sense of creation and perfect achievement, that corresponds to the sense of satisfaction which pervades one's whole person when one has correctly solved a problem or said an illuminating word.

What is the source of these unsubstantial curving forms that move, objective to consciousness, in weaving bands of color? To the best of my knowledge and belief, they do not originate in my own consciousness, either as memories or as imagination. I have said that they occur in an objectivity that is non-materialistic. This I believe to be true. And the only non-materialistic objective realm of which we have any conception is a possible universal mind, a possible universal consciousness.

We know that, philosophically, there exists a human mental realm in which the *form* of each man-made thing comes into being before its substantial shape is constructed or otherwise produced. In these regions of the human mind, ideas, thoughts, and images come and go, dawn and pass, sometimes in a long-drawn-out process. What immaterial history lies behind the first pitcher? What factors of knowledge, imagination, aspiration, will, memory, hope—and fear—were synthesized into form in Cellini's mind before his "Perseus" became a physical fact in the world? It was out of the elements and essences of his psychological being that that new thing, marvelous and beautiful, was created—a product of mental ideation translated into substance.

The realms of mind are not confined within men's skulls. But within the psychic nature of humanity there is an affinity with, and the means for perceiving, the fluid flow of the endless fantasy of the universe. Someone has said that the only portion of the divine mind that we can know is its subconscious. As with ourselves, that subconscious is a moving, ever-present flow of the experienced—not destroyed, dead, and gone, but forever reenacting itself in fantasy, in accordance with the laws by which universal nature continues to exist.

I can give no better impression of my sense and my belief than by saying that the stream of imagery which I perceive in telepathy is the shifting fantasy occurring in the divine subconscious of the universe. And as, in our dreams, some stimulus will produce, out of our subconscious content, a sequential though irrational drama of persons, circumstances, and events which touches the edge of our awareness, our wonder, and our understanding, so in the great subconscious of the universe there proceeds the constant play of divine fantasy, significant also to the psychic perception of mankind.

To me this does not seem to be a metaphysical idea simply, but a psychological fact. And I am tempted to pursue it a step further, from the psychological point of view. If, in the absence of my conscious awareness, as in sleep, the sensory stimulus of a light, a sound, or a touch can stir my subconscious to the depth where a particular type of fantasy-performance eventuates, so that I perceive at the edge of awareness a dramatic incident which may have happened to me far away and long ago—even in the primitive past of Lévy-Brühl's *participation mystique*—how can I deny, or even question, the reality and significance of the symbols which I telepathically perceive in the field of the universal mind that is available to man?

I conceive the sensory experience of each moment as entering into the content of my subconscious and in some measure qualifying it. Thus the mass of my subconscious has been accumulated, and this is the source of my purposeless fantasy. But above the subconscious there are areas of the mind which work with purposes that transcend both the play of the sensory perceptions and the flow of fantasy; this is the human area of creative and synthetic forms. And beyond this mental phase—objective to it in a non-sensory direction—there is the world of psychic relationships, the world in which our highest consciousness capacity becomes aware of phases of the universal subconscious.

Since these matters are subtle, any attempt to explain or discuss them in terms that will carry clarity tends to give an impression of heaviness in the theme itself. As a matter of fact, however, the super-sensory activities are experiences of a superior lightness. Having come into the supersensory state, one is singularly concentrated, alert, poised, and attentive (but without curiosity)—like the well-trained setter poised above the birds; and one watches the symbolic flow of color and form with an acutely focused interest, in which there is neither strain nor tension, but rather a high sense of newly achieved and limitless freedom.

It is significant too that one returns to the conscious sensory world unfatigued, which seems to indicate that in the supersensory activities one has not simply spent one's energies abroad, but that, instead, one has made contact with sources of energy that are superior to one's own, and has drawn from them, into oneself, new draughts of refreshment and vitality. The true psychic experience leaves one with the impression, after the event, that one has actually participated in the activities of a state of being which transcends our ordinary human state.

We can thus understand without difficulty the experience of the religious mystics who achieve to various high levels of union with Divinity. The whole of the individual consciousness is at once merged and flooded with the transcendent vitality of identity with the One; and the descent from that state is a descent indeed, involving a loss so great that the experience has been called the dark night of the soul.

In this chapter, as in the whole book, I have endeavored to be clearly and cogently explanatory; but I have referred to the emotional content which is necessarily an element in the essence of super-sensory experience, and this emotional factor is qualitatively much more important than is generally indicated in what I have written. Our deepest emotional and mental experiences are always difficult, if not impossible, to translate into adequate terms for the eye or the ear to gather. Therefore I am adding here a page or two, set down without any attempt at sequence, as a passage purely impressionistic, with bits of graphic accompaniment ...

A large leaf, fronds stiff and straight, reaching into light—a picture of the spinal column's relation to the body. In times of illness in the past the fronds wilted when I had temperature. This leaf supplies numerous images which store a fluid reserve ...

I am sure that each symbol is specially related to some seat of function in the body. They represent the guiding lines, the cleavages of relationship in the subjective working together of the inner bodies. If I am emotionally disturbed, *they* are disturbed in their movements of free flowing and free forming—like stars confused to my sight by drifting clouds. In contemplative calm, they are the silent guardians and representatives of a primal peace.

All the symbols are at their best when there is well poised work to be done. Then they move like under-water growths, in shimmering light and glowing color, with easy and undisturbed grace, repeatedly enfolding and releasing each other, like the finely synchronized movements of a well-run machine.

I am aware of them thus in times of contemplation. They turn in on themselves gracefully and with infinite subtlety, like the swift, lithe movements of a fairy dance. At the beginning of the day's work they move upward and outward, inducing animation and holding it. They are never disturbing, never intrusive. I banish them as I become objective, attentive, and aware. Yet I imagine that if I did not know they are always with me I might have been disturbed at times by the flow of fantasy they produce . . .

I believe that my early child life, filled with introspection and long silences, as I waited in suspense for the inside of things to be revealed, gave me the key to my own inner subjective workings. So did I discover my own key to life, without understanding its meaning. My picture-language led me into a world, later, where I am able to observe the mechanisms of myself and my relationships at work.

There are five basic symbols that I feel are fundamentally related to the five senses. I become very deeply aware of these if and when any of the senses are called upon or affected in an emotional way.

At an early age I accepted the yew tree and put it in a very special place where it stood behind and "filled in" with other images. I can call upon and command it in melancholy moods or in deep emotion. When I am strained or tired and find in it the will to obey me, I am certain that it is not simply a part of my own private imagery.

It forms itself into the III or I, as the sticks of a fan open and close. This III or I, in either form, is a basic I, and it expresses inherent will. I think of this particular symbol with respect ... Sometimes it splits itself, becoming a panel (this differs from the fan) through which light lines curl. It often sways in long rhythmic movement like the outline of the U or the O, if one can imagine such a motion as swift and long at the same time. The O is never quite completely closed. When the yew tree joins itself with the light lines it can take a form suggesting the swastika, ⚝ yet different, since it turns in on itself recedingly. This is also an old Mayan form. It takes on shapes reminiscent of a shell ⟑ or a numeral ⟑ None of these forms is ever finished; they never finally complete themselves. They are not forms only, but movement also; it is difficult to indicate the sequential flow ... And they do not appear singly, but sometimes in profusion. They gather and coalesce and disappear kaleidoscopically: ∭ ⫻ At times the yew tree will appear suddenly, as if by magic within magic.

The form of the O is never quite closed, and there is a corresponding form 𝓒 that I think of as a magic circle which embraces, yet leaves free, whatever appears within it. To me it signifies free association, and I have a sense of impersonal uplift and development when it appears—a sense of responsibility that is capable of whatever it may undertake.

In my symbolic field nothing is ever closed, finished, ended; nothing stands still or by itself alone. All that appears is in process of movement, like a phase in a creative act. And though the forms disappear, they leave a feeling, a knowing, that they participate in other action, wherever they may be ...

The yew tree is "the Watcher." At night, or in the calm of morning, the Watcher is like a white flame, a pale finger upraised. It thus becomes the center of the I, a fundamental image in this fluid imagery. In movement the primary I becomes III, as though a gateway. The Watcher, I, weaving and spinning, gathers impetus; and, never alone, it gathers shapes and moves in rhythms ... These are sometimes akin to the letters of the alphabet:

$$A\ B\ L$$

Such shapes, in their swift mobility, limn flowing pictures, quickly, yet easily, without hurry ...

The symbolism then is an expression of unspoken, unrevealed thought. It is the keeper of the thought, so to speak, through which the light threads drift, weaving themselves into significance for comprehension.

These are all subjective symbols, of course. As the meanings of words change with successive generations, and languages lose their original values, may it not be that these inner symbols protect the very form of consciousness against its own erratic wandering and diffusion?

The keeper of the thought will sometimes change

and become an inner pair of pools, like inner eyes, azure blue, through which one sees into the depths beyond the self. I associate these pools with clear seeing—clairvoyance. Invariably, in these pools other images shape themselves and take on forms that are related to the sun, the moon, and the stars. It often comes to me that bodies have a planetary weather of their own, subject to the suns and moons and other planets and galaxies of their several synthetic integrations. Elsewhere I mention the relation of the liver to the sun, in this internal cosmos, and the relation of the heart to the moon ...

Most perfect of the images is the spiral, forever moving and forming within and out of itself. I see within the spiral the development of all energy; it is the symbol of growth in space. As it moves and creates form within itself, it is an enduring symbol, evolving and involving forms that flow and shape themselves into other forms—all of them together participating in the constant creation of still other symbolic images which, in being born, follow a whirling movement as they escape swiftly from the bright threads of the spiral, to take on their own movement and meaning …

When I first went to school, as a little girl, I had great difficulty in learning to write. A large chart of the alphabet, capitals and small letters, hung on the schoolroom wall. Never in the experience of my whole life have I encountered anything else so remote from my interest, so lacking in stimulus and meaning, as those unnatural black shapes standing rigid in rows and columns on a white ground. I was expected to learn them—the letters—their names, "the sounds they made." But they made no sounds, and they evoked no subtle sounds in me.

I also had a copy book in which the fifty-two forms were repeated—or so I was told. But actually they were not the same shapes at all. It was painstakingly explained to me that A on the chart and *A* in my copy book were the same letter and had the same sound— "aye." The B on the chart and the *B* in my copy book were also said to be alike, as were the C and the *C* and so forth. Yet to my sense, the two halves of each pair differed radically, and I just could not grasp the necessity or the art involved in having four different shapes for the sound "dee."

I can still recall the very few spots of affinity that seemed to exist between the alphabet and me. There were the B-b-*B-b*; I knew what a bee was, but it was none of these. C-c-*C-c*; I knew what the sea was, but I found no relation between these letters and salt water, though the sound of their names was the same. F-f-*F-f* were not "if" badly sounded. I-i-*I-i* were, amazingly, me. J-j-*J-j*; I knew a jay was a bird. O-o-*O-o*; these seemed to me beautiful, for they were a kind of pattern, if one put them together. It was through the round peep-hole of the O, I believe, that I glimpsed my first inkling of sense in the whole matter. P-p-*P-p*—we had peas in the garden. U-u-*U-u* meant "You," and W-w-*W-w*—meant you and somebody else.

As I struggled to understand, finding no real sympathy in my difficulty, I became aware that this was one of those strange things that *had to be done*, and I began to attempt to reproduce the copy-book models as I was expected to.

Here I met a further distress, for the letters that I made did not resemble the copy-book models—not in the least. I could neither reduce my copies to the restricted scope of the originals nor sustain the continuity of their beautiful curves. It was almost as though, for me, a single line was purely negative, non-existent, impossible. I had to give volume to my representations, and the only way in which I could do this was to repeat each stroke of the letter that I tried to form: *C U P*

In those early days the whole matter was an affair of nightmare, discipline, and readjustment, but I have since come to realize how the dancing inner lines of light, the flowing bands of color, had conditioned me. The lines of light always appeared in series, and they were so *real*—so vital and *natural*—that that was how things should be, from my point of view. I was used to receiving meanings directly from the symbols I saw, and this without tension or strain ...

It was through the vowels that I eventually saw behind these strange black symbols on white paper, and thus found my way into written English. I and U and 0—these were my seeds of illumination. And it has come to me since that this is wholly natural, for the vowels are the open sounds, and this is psychologically significant. They are vital, to my sense, involving direct inhalation and exhalation of the fundamental breath; thus directly affecting the lungs, the heart, the blood-flow, the whole metabolism of the body; they are basic to our entire means of expression.

I have, of course, learned to write the alphabet, and to perform many other learned techniques; yet the inner world of symbols, perceived and felt, is still present and fundamentally significant, whenever I turn awareness to it. It represents the very essence of vitality—energy bursting into form at a level which, for us, is primal.

IX
Perception and Communication

I WAS A SENSITIVE CHILD full of dreams. In the earliest days of which I have any recollection, I lived in two worlds, of which one was my own. It was definitely my own world, because none of the other human beings about me had any conception of or sympathy with it. That I could see the wind, apprehend the inner individuality of trees and flowers and animals, perceive the "surrounds"—those misty, multicolored envelopes in which all living objects moved, which changed with their moods or the changing conditions of their lives—that I could foretell at times the occurrence of events which later actually came to pass, and that I had an understanding of people which was penetratingly intuitive and often belied the impressions which they endeavored to create by spoken words or physical gestures and attitudes—all this cut me off in a large measure from the surface life of my environment, and repeatedly drew me into the free, bright states of consciousness where I could be with the lovely natural sights and sounds and events of my own infinitely better world.

It was a wholly natural world. Its denizens lived their lives, not without conflict; but there were no pretenses or deceptive artificialities of conduct here, no submission to rules and laws that cramped and inhibited the normal process of life.

Hearing the various sounds of growth in the vegetable world, watching the weavings of wind and water, listening to the expressions of the fowls and animals as they performed the activities of their busy lives, I was carefree, but acutely conscious and interested and happy. I repeatedly rebelled against the commanding forms and pressures that strove to draw me away from this freedom, and I resented (but learned to accept) the specious reasoning that was used to justify my disciplining and my unhappiness.

Life has changed for me in many ways as the years have passed; but I have never lost the way into my own bright early world. My faculties of perception are not now the same as they were in those early days. Knowledge, understanding, and sympathy have developed as the results of countless events and experiences, and above everything, perhaps, *I have learned deeply not to resist life*. There *is* a destiny that shapes our ends. It is hidden as a pattern or model deep within each one of us. To resist it, for any reason but service, is to induce sufferings for which there is no warrant. Accepting his inner destiny, man may suffer too, and even more acutely; but he will

99

then be conforming to nature according to his own destiny; he will be living fully in life and fulfilling himself. Incidentally, I believe this to be a primary credential for the continuity of one's development after death.

The years which elapsed between my childhood and my marriage were not spectacular in any way. When, at the age of sixteen, I left Ireland, I bade good-by to all the intimate friends I had among the trees and flowers and animals, and I did so with a premonitory feeling that I should never again be as happy in life as I had been in those early conditions. London and marriage followed, and presently my husband objected to my "visioning" and "sensing people and things in my own old way. Assuring me that other people did not see and sense things as I did, he warned me that my capacities held many aspects that were commonly considered to be the elements of insanity. I was very young, and it was a time of great anxiety for me; but I could no more negate seeing and sensing things as I did than the sun can cease its shining. I had my own double world to live in; and if it was different from the world in which other people lived, what could I do?

I finally solved the problem by dividing my time and my life and my consciousness. As occasion demanded, I was a bright and cordial wife, conforming to the conventions, ready and eager to share my husband's life. When I was alone I was myself, happy and free in a state where no one could reach me, to hurt or confuse me. And I came to the point of telling myself that if this private condition was a phase of insanity, then I had no fear of insanity—this was the condition of life that I needed and wanted.

In the years that followed I bore three sons who died in their infancy. The birth of these small creatures into the world, and their so quickly passing out of it, affected me variously. Both before and after the birth of my first son I seemed to be unified and completed within myself in a manner which was not repeated with the other children. Following the deaths of my first and second boys within a few months of each other, I was deeply shaken and ill. I had watched the nebulous thread of life weave upward and away from those small forms as I held them in my arms; and though I already knew that death is not an end of human existence, I was downcast, depressed, and unhappy in their loss. Following my first son's birth, I had been warned by a voice, speaking behind me, that he would not be in this world very long, and turning to see who had spoken, I found no one there …

I wanted intensely to follow my dead sons, not by dying myself, but to discover and know just what happened to them, just what condition they were experiencing beyond the interlude of their brief visit here. And though I could not follow them very far, the intensity of my desire to do so seemed to occasion some further development in my own nature, for I began to penetrate the outer sheaths and see into the depths of dense forms. I no longer perceived light and color in rays or beams, but as weaving streams that curved and rotated and spiraled endlessly into space. I learned to travel along these lines, out into space, into a mental world of exhilaration and light. I also began to sense and feel the thoughts of other people, and I learned that thoughts are things, possessing their own vitality, their own destiny for ill or good.

It was in this period also that I became aware of a division that occurred in my own unity. I was one day surprised and disturbed to perceive a shadowy replica of myself at some distance in front of me. After observing it for a moment I rose from my chair and attempted to approach that alter ego, and as I did so it lost outline and drew back toward me. It was my own "surround." I have since learned that it could be expanded, and I have found out many other things about the qualities of surrounds—my own and other people's; but that was the first experience of unconscious "projection" I had ever had.

I sometimes *saw* (and still do see) through a strange sensitivity in my finger-tips and the nape of my neck, far more clearly than with my eyes. Sound came to me in a current from without, washed my whole body like a wave, and vibrated in the bony structure of my person, so that I *heard* in my feet and in my knees. And I still hear with my feet and my fingers.

Then events occurred which marked the beginning of a new order for me. I needed to get away from myself and work because, as always, of a terrific inner need. And the opportunity came for me to go into business with a friend. I worked hard, and the consequent daily weariness of my body brought me sleep—which meant rest for my mind and my nervous system, the energy of which I yet hardly understood.

My aunt died, in Ireland, and I suddenly realized that I was free for the first time in my life. In my childhood, this aunt had been the dominating representative of a culture which had crystallized into a rigidity of convention and which was constantly opposed to my need of freedom. She condemned my parentage and my own inner nature; and though she honestly meant, according to her lights, to save me from myself, she made the attempt without tenderness, beauty, or finesse. Even after I escaped from her direct tutelage, I suffered the indelible shadow of her influence. Now, at last, my life was freed from its principal incubus forever.

I was thus free and busy when the First World War started. My husband, who was a Territorial, was detailed to duty abroad. During his absence, I looked after his house and attended to my own business commitments. But I presently found that I was pregnant, and in due time my daughter was born. For several months after her birth, I was dangerously ill. My lungs have never since been strong. And, due to an accumulation of circumstances about which I have written elsewhere,* I decided to end our marriage when

---

* In Eileen J. Garrett (1939). *My Life as the Search for the Meaning of Mediumship.* New York: Oquaga Press.

my husband returned to England, and this I did.

I had always known, subjectively, that I must some day create my own way and my own work in the world, and with my nervous difficulties largely adjusted through the hard work and regular discipline of a full life, I looked forward with eagerness to rearing my daughter and developing my own career.

The war was still in progress. I was managing the officers' hostel which I had opened in London, and though that work took much of my time and energy, I still found, when I was alone, that my *seeing* and *sensing* were developing into other types of perception. I began to be conscious of episodes and fragments of incidents that flashed before me like blurred pictures on a screen. They were pictures of people whom I knew and people I did not know. Later I met some of the people I had first beheld in this visionary way. Or I might read in the day's newspaper of a fire, an explosion, or some other event of which I had had a prevision that day, or several days before. Those new sensitivities were accompanied by physical effects corresponding to the reactions I would have suffered if I had been present at the actual event, and I was deeply distressed at the thought that my nervous instability of the past might be returning.

I had been married again—for little more than a month. And through that relationship I had the shattering experience, in London, of participating in the violent death of my husband, in France. I had gone in the evening to dine and dance with some friends; and at half past eleven the vision of my husband's disaster began to develop. I lost my sense of myself and became involved in a terrific explosion. When I recovered my sense of my own identity, I was sitting alone in the hotel foyer, and knew in my conscious mind that my husband was dead.

A few days later word came from the War Office confirming the fact. He had been killed at Ypres.

That present developmental phase was a strain in every aspect of my life. I knew, then, beyond question, that I was receiving impressions of events occurring in various distances of time and space. Each of those events had its deep effect on my mind and my nervous system; and under those disruptive impacts I was apprehensive of what was happening to me psychologically. I had never heard of psychic prevision, and though I had had the experience of fore-knowing as a child, I had since acquired clear conceptions of what were considered "normal" and "abnormal." In the earlier years, my previsioning had been like the natural objective perception of any fact—as one might, for instance, note a particular tree in a landscape. Now, however, I was not only perceiving distant and often disastrous events, but was also involved and participating in them. I was repeatedly affected by personalities and events to which I was related in a manner that was not only incomprehensible and mysterious, but disruptive.

In my attempts to understand the situation and to find the means for protecting myself from these disruptive effects, I followed two main lines of self-treatment. First, as I had always done before in times of crisis, I deliberately and consciously called upon the Breath of the Universe to help me to build up some strength, some power of control, which would enable me to shut myself away and to escape from the shattering effects of these visionary participations. And second, as I lay in bed, I would consciously and firmly demand of the several divisions of my mind—as I had learned to differentiate them—that they resist the intrusion of these external events upon my consciousness.

I was naturally aware, by this time, that there were two selves within me, conscious and subconscious. Realizing deeply the acute needs of my life, I corrected conditions that were adverse by consciously instructing my subconscious. This was a technique of autosuggestion; and I noted that so long as I continued the practice, the irresistible invasion of outer events subsided, while if I gave it up for a time, the invasion would again occur.

So it became habitual with me to perform nightly my self-protective ritual of suggestion. As I came to appreciate the success of the process I began to experiment with it for the control of illness and pain, and for the management of the events and relationships of my daily life. In the whole process, I gradually gained freedom from the dominance of my visioning capacity, so that I was no longer merely its victim. I had not lost the capacity, but had learned to control it. I could now permit it to operate, or I could inhibit it. I accepted the fact that my inner mind held a second faculty of perception that was not dependent on the senses; and whatever significances the world might find in this fact could make no difference to me—this was the condition of consciousness with which I had to find a way to live.

Nevertheless I had to understand for myself the nature of this extra capacity, and as I experimented with it as time went on, it broadened in scope. I understood as a primary fact that, controlled instead of controlling, it had no disastrous effects upon my life. It also had incidental elements of interest, for I might at times become aware of a brief bit of sensed conversation which, a few days later, I would hear vocally repeated in some group or gathering in which I was present. Names of unknown people and places would often catch my attention as they passed in my mind, and days or weeks or years later these names and people and places would come into some normal factual relation to my life.

I also learned at this time that not only was the more or less remote outer world affecting my consciousness, but I was affecting the outer world, without directly intending to do so. Friends sometimes wrote to ask about me because they had been impressed by so positive a sense of my presence in their houses that they were disturbed, and had been moved to get in communication with me. I was usually able to coordinate such cases with the fact that I had been thinking of these friends while in a passive state of mind; and eventually I came to realize that in such circumstances one part of my mind went out and reached their subtle sensibilities. Later, when I became familiar with the mechanics of telepathy and clairvoyance, I learned to project this second part of my mind to places and persons, not by chance, but directly and purposively.

As time went on I became aware of sensations behind my eyes, at the root of my nose, and in my forehead, as though a physical channel were being opened up between a center in my forehead and the cerebellum. My visioning increased in clarity, and I finally became clearly conscious of a spot in the forehead, between the eyebrows, as the center where the images began to register. This process of registering images was one in which energy seemed to move outward from this center in my forehead and to focus at a point that was far distant from me—though this "distance" was an effect in consciousness rather than in space.

As I strove to understand these various developments in my life, I evolved a philosophy out of my own experience. Primarily, I became aware of the infinite variety of facts and possibilities of consciousness that exist in the universe, beyond the little realm of the finite individual mind. I came to know, for myself, that human lives and human minds are parts of the universal life and mind; that this universal life is evolving; and that the individual human being participates in this evolutionary process according to his capacity and his will to do so.

As my capacity came into contact with the practical world, I progressively realized that the focus of most people's consciousness is reversed. They are all continually trying to remodel the universe to the pattern of their own diverse purposes. I noted how responsibility, success, money, or environment tended to change the freedom and fire of individual devotions. I observed how authority tended to crystallize into self-importance, letting vital purposes wait. As I came into contact with leaders of various movements, I was often disappointed to find them over-conscious of their own importance and insufficiently concerned with the ideals of the movements which they represented. Ideals seemed to be dissipated by the means that were instituted to express them. The shadow of individuality repeatedly blotted out the clear brightness of the larger issue.

The war had now ended, and in the post-war period I found a friend, Edward Carpenter. There is an aphorism in the East which says that when the student is ready the teacher will appear. Having come to certain conceptions of my own in relation to the universal, evidently I was now ready for the help of Edward Carpenter's knowledge and wisdom. He understood all of my past experiences, and regretted that I had not had some understanding person to encourage and stand by me in my times of difficulty. In reference to religious sects and dogmas, he said, "I have my own God. And so have you." He directed my study and reading, and discussed with me my reactions to philosophies, experiences, and books.

In the two years of my friendship with Edward Carpenter, I experienced a profound mental and spiritual expansion of my life. Through this expansion, I was completely freed from the sense of the past and came to the recognition of my own integrity. He verified my sense of what he called the Cosmic Consciousness, and made me understand that my visioning and sensing were not the effects of mental unbalance, but were positive powers, anciently recognized, for knowing and understanding realities beyond the range of ordinary comprehension.

I have said that a voice had warned me that my first son would not be long in this world. Now my daughter was ill with her first serious illness. I had heard the doctor report that he could do nothing more, and I desperately resolved in my own mind that I would not give up the fight for my child's life. I sent the nurse away, and decided positively that my daughter must get well. I lifted her out of her bed as she gasped for breath, and desperately held her close to my body, to give her of my own strength ... A voice behind me said, "Be careful. She must have more air. Open the window and allow a new current of air in the room." I opened the window, saw the curtain flutter, and, turning, I saw the outline of a figure leaning against the bed—a short, lithe man whose face was turned from me. Though my limbs were trembling, I approached the bed and laid my daughter down. The man in gray garments stood beside me with a sympathetic smile. I did not know who he was, but I did know that he had come to help me save the child's life. He presently disappeared, without my seeing him go. My daughter did recover. She is now a healthy, happy, married woman.

Later I came into contact with Spiritism. At first I was perturbed to learn that the Spiritists believed death to involve a change of existence in time and space, but not a change in individual consciousness. I had my own ideas concerning the continuity of existence after death, yet I could not define them precisely. In a spirit of inquiry and experimentation, I joined a spiritualist society, attended meetings, read books, and listened to countless "experiences" of numerous people. I joined a group that gathered for psychic development, and at one of our meetings, something unexpected happened. I felt drowsy and fell into sleep. When I awoke, the other members of the group, much agitated, told me that I had given evidence of the presence of their dead relatives and friends—entities who spoke to them all.

In consequence of this occurrence, I met Mr. Huhnli, a Swiss, who was kind and helpful. He asked me what had happened, and when I told him, he suggested that I sit quietly and relax. Again I became sleepy and lost consciousness, and when I awoke, Mr. Huhnli told me I was a potential trance medium of considerable power. In trance, it seemed, a condition was created in which, while I was unconscious, some other intelligence might enter and take control of my organism, and use it as a means for communication. This had happened in the sitting, and Mr. Huhnli had talked with my first "control," an Oriental, who gave his name as Uvani.

I was frightened by this whole development, and made up my mind to forget all of these experiences and go away, possibly to Australia, in order to break the whole pattern of my past and have the stimulation of a fresh environment. But this was not to be. In spite of my inner resistances, I found myself continuing my associations with people who were interested in Spiritism, and finally I met Hewat McKenzie.

McKenzie had founded the British College of Psychic Science. He was a great help to me, clarifying my ideas on the significances of psychic activities as a whole, assuring me that I had no need to fear the invasion of my personality by any control, and explaining that one of the principal values of mediumship lay in the development of the control personalities so that they might become adequate and useful communicators. In the course of time, and under Mr. McKenzie's guidance, I built up a reputation as a trance medium at the British College of Psychic Science; and in doing so I shut away all the other aspects of psychic experience.

Hewat McKenzie's death, in 1929, removed the loftiest exemplar of the Spiritist faith and understanding with whom I had come in contact. Without his example and precept to sustain me, my own inner doubts of the value of the mediumistic work I was doing—doubts based mainly on the futility of most of the communicated material—became dominant in my life. I felt a personal responsibility to my "sitters," and also for the effects and consequences of the communications for which I provided the channel.

In the midst of these uncertainties, I was again ill and had two serious operations, so that I was in bed for months. It was then that I began to realize the magnetic potencies that constantly surround us, and to experiment with them, and with color, for their healing values. And I learned in some measure, during this time, to revitalize myself.

Just prior to this long period of illness, I had been informed that a new control had spoken through me to some of my sitters. His name was Abdul Latif. It was a name I had never heard before, though he was known to have communicated through other mediums. The substance of his communications was very different from the substance of Uvani's. Uvani had spent his time steadily, for years, in giving evidence of "survival"; but Abdul Latif was a healer and a prophet, a teacher and a philosopher in spiritual terms. He has stated that in his life on earth he was a Persian astronomer and physician connected with the court of Saladin, in the time of the Crusades.

I have thus briefly summarized my life, up to this point, in order to acquaint the reader with some of the main phases of the process of my psychic development. There were further steps in the process. But with the advent of a second control to use my trance, I became deeply concerned about the whole technique of communication and the actual nature of the controls.

During the years, I have submitted to many types of medical and psychological examination in an endeavor to determine the exact nature and source of the controls, but thus far without satisfactory results. During the days when I worked with Hewat McKenzie, I submitted to his hypnotism and allowed him to "train" the control, who was then Uvani; but I was never completely convinced in my own consciousness that Uvani was a separate integrated entity who operated from another plane of consciousness. Hewat McKenzie had always attached much importance to the strength of the subconscious; yet when I spoke to him about this uncertainty in my mind, and suggested that instead of being a distinct personality Uvani might simply be a split-off of my own subconscious, he was indignant.

I had every confidence in the genuineness of Mr. and Mrs. McKenzie's faith and private assurance; yet for my own assurance I needed further evidence, which was not forthcoming. I simply did not know within myself that the controls were in fact what they were commonly supposed to be.

When Abdul Latif began to speak through my trance, therefore, the situation became more acute; for if Uvani represented a possible split in my subconscious mind—a condition that was stressed by analysts and others—this second control might represent a second split-off, and both of them might possibly be symptoms of a general disintegration of my personality. For me, the problem involved both the validity of the controls and the integrity of my own private nature.

During one of the most serious crises of my life, when I was in hospital with both a burst appendix and an infected mastoid, the doctors and nurses in the operating room heard a voice speaking, just after I had become unconscious under the anesthetic. What the voice said was not known, since it evidently spoke in a strange language; but I was later told by G. R. S. Mead, who often communicated with Abdul Latif through my trance, that the control had informed him that he had himself been in the operating room at that time.

The problem of the reality of the control personalities was not merely personal or superficial for me, and it presently became even more acute; for on returning to work, after my illness, I found that I could not produce satisfactory results. After ten years of successful work as a sensitive, what had happened to dissolve that well-trained capacity and disrupt its relationships? Whatever had happened had happened to me. It was of course possible that my own loss of faith would have had something to do with the changed situation, if an established conviction had ever been a sure basis of the successful work I had done. But I had never had such a firm conviction …

There was also another aspect of my generally confused and dissatisfied state. While I had never fully accepted the controls as conscious individualized entities, I had a high measure of faith—born of experience and conviction—in both the reality and the high nature of some source as the place of origination of the material that was transmitted through my trance. In the case of Uvani, were "the dead" the actual source of his transmitted messages?

I was inwardly quite clear concerning both ends of the process of trance communication—a high source of supersensory knowledge, and the genuineness of the material which was communicated. What perplexed and disturbed me was the middle term, the *process*. I could no longer submit to this activity automatically, on faith alone; I had to *know* what I was doing.

These problems continued to disturb me for several years, during which time my faith in the processes was so uncertain that, though my trance again became a competent channel for communication by the controls, it was almost impossible for me to cooperate in communicating with "the dead." I can only suppose that this inability was the result of some inhibitory alteration occurring in my own nature. Since my early childhood, I had been aware of sound, movement, color, and vitality in forms that other people did not sense. These early faculties had developed, and I could now see clairvoyantly, hear clairaudiently, and sense telepathically; yet I did not know *how* these perceptive capacities operated, and I was intensely interested in finding out.

After much experience and much research, I do not yet clearly know the nature of trance. I am convinced, however, and ready to state as a definite conclusion, that clairvoyance and telepathy depend upon some natural active radiation that is created between two people or between an individual and an object. This radiation may be reciprocated between them mutually, or it may operate only in one direction. But I am convinced that there must be established between them, across time and space, a relationship so definite and so affective that it amounts to a stimulus, for the clairvoyant, at least—a stimulus of interest, necessity, or will sufficient to divert energy and consciousness from the sensory field and to concentrate them in the areas of super-sensory perception. Supersensory perception is not limited, as the sensory perceptions are, by time and space. It operates in a clear field—a field which, at its own level, is never interrupted or discontinuous. And in that field, it finds a mutualistic response or receptivity in the object of its stimulated search.

It will perhaps be interesting if I mention, in passing, that hypnotism, telepathy, clairvoyance, and certain other capacities are occultly supposed to occur in the "astral plane," which lies "next beyond" our normal plane of conscious living. Theoretically, the astral is the plane of cosmic memory, where images of all beings and past events are preserved. There the prototypes of future creations are also present, awaiting their birth into the world of form and action. Has trance some direct relation to such areas?

During 1934, I cooperated in some tests made by Dr. William Brown, a well-known English psychiatrist who founded the experimental laboratory of psychology at Oxford. I had less than a dozen appointments with Dr. Brown, most of the work being done under hypnosis. As the work was inadequate, in any scientific sense, I need not go into the details of the experiments. I want to say, however, that while I was under hypnosis, Dr. Brown never succeeded in reaching the controls, though he did speak with Uvani, at the last appointment, while I was in trance.

But in these sessions with Dr. Brown I learned the method by which he had been able to make me recall, on waking from the hypnotic state, exactly what I had said under hypnosis. I felt that I could perhaps apply a similar method of hypnotic suggestion to myself. If I had been able to speak under the suggestion of hypnotic control, could I not definitely affect myself by written suggestion? I felt that if I gave myself the necessary suggestion before going into trance, I might be able to penetrate to the levels of consciousness that were open to the trance "controls," and I felt that my automatic writing would probably reveal facts concerning those levels.

Thus it happened, in the course of time and practice, that a new force or capability began to appear in my supersensory functioning. I developed an ability to penetrate to the levels of consciousness from which the controls drew their supernormal knowledge. Penetration of these areas made me aware of a consciousness greater than anything I had ever conceived, imagined, or experienced. I became individually lost and vibrant in awareness itself. I was permitted to perceive and *know* from the realms of some ultimate source that existed beyond all the reaches of conscious personal being ...

The controls were not in evidence in this experience, yet they were not displaced or dissipated by it. I still continue to act as intermediary for the communications of controls. And I have also become convinced that my trance does not represent some strange or unique faculty, but is rather the developed and integrated extension of capacities possessed by all men, along those little-known corridors of being which unite the individual to the universal.

We are accustomed to thinking of the whole process of perception as an effect upon the sensory capacities from without, which, through nervous sensitivity, causes an impression in the brain, resulting in the evocation of an image in the mind. To this image the organism reacts more or less positively, according to the nature and quality of both of them and according to the nature of the relation between them. Such images are not fixed in type; they do not represent unequivocal clear reflections of the affective object or condition, but are the response of a qualified, synthetic, and constantly changing condition of being to symbolic impressions.

If we consider the processes of reflective thought, we observe that they consist of the fluid procession, in the mind, of images which, instead of being sensorily evoked, evoke one another. This is the most common area of nonsensory perception, and it is the most obvious area of man's mentation beyond the dominance of sensory effect. Supposing such a thought-process to be aimed at the solution of a problem or the development of a seed idea, it becomes creative in the measure in which the aim is achieved. Selective decisions of acceptance and rejection of various images are made on the way to fulfillment. Physically, emotionally, and mentally, the organism is then unified and concentrated in the areas of supersensory creative activity.

If we consider the human organism in its practice of meditation, prayer, loyalty, devotion, and love, we find it operating in areas still further removed from the conditions of sensory effect, and perceptive of symbols (often acquired) the qualities of which transcend, in significance and universalism, the analytical and critical capacities of the sense-trained mind.

It is at this point, beyond mental capacity, that faith displaces understanding, that aspiration rises above knowledge born of sensory and rational experience. Both this faith and this aspiration are experience, too; and if they are sufficiently practiced and repeated, they progressively qualify the consciousness—progressively, because in this direction, as in any other direction on which the human consciousness is consistently concentrated, eventual awareness, through supersensory perception, definitely colors the psychic content of the individual.

Here, as in the field of reflective thought, the images which repeatedly enter the field of perception come to have relative values of their own. As in direct sensory perception, in dreams, in mental ideation, so here, the sensed stimulus is clothed in imagery by the qualified capacity of the psyche, and the mystic knows what he knows.

It is thus obvious that both perception and awareness occur in supersensory fields. That faith is a normal way of life is also obvious, for in entering on any new line of inquiry or knowledge, we have to trust to the symbolism of the book or the instructor. In each beginning these symbols are incomprehensible; but through repeated effect, sensorily or otherwise received, consciousness creatively synthesizes its imagery into significances that are related to the values that lie behind the symbolism. In this process one may eventually become highly versed in the theory of medicine or business or mechanics. This translation of theories into practice (action) is a different field.

The natural psychic is one who possesses a natural sensitivity of perception in certain directions. For him, the field of supersensory perception is relatively a line of least resistance. Usually, in the beginning at least, he becomes aware of his sensitivity through some phenomenal operation of the psychic capacity. From that beginning, he is either adequately instructed or he follows his own experimental method of development. Most of the psychic power in the world is wasted because, in my opinion, our current culture does not know how to make use of it. By our education and environment, we are all curtailed, more or less, on the subtle side of life; our education and environment have led us away from the areas of psychic perception and experience.

I think, however, that the leading civilized peoples are now standing at the very fringes of psychic appreciation. What we have to achieve, primarily and unequivocally, are the realization and acceptance of a whole new set of values. These values are apt to impress the rational mind, trained in the recent world-school, as visionary and impractical; but a brief unprejudiced view of the world-history of the past hundred years will indicate how denaturalized we have become through over-concentration on materialistic lines of thought and action. A reaction toward a more truly *human* norm seems now to be in the air. This does not mean that the world is going "psychic," by and large; but it probably does mean that we are going to begin to emerge from the chaos which our materialistic obsession has created in the life of mankind as a whole, and to realize that human life-values do transcend the areas of value represented by the sensory field. Thoughts are things. Objective, superpersonal thinking is a capacity which cannot be denied by humanity without the disruption, and possibly the loss, of its humanism. Humanism, however, is the distinguishing and saving mark of social man. The present world conflict is being fought out on these very questions of saving man's achieved humanism and extending it.

X
The Way Inward

IN AN EARLIER BOOK,* I have recorded the repeated physical break-downs that I suffered in the past. Several times I approached very close to death. But I was never afraid, because at the inner center of myself there lay a germ of conviction, of realization, of knowledge that I had not yet completed or fulfilled the purpose of my existence. Although I had been working as a trance-medium for several years, I was thus engaging in an activity the significances of which I did not altogether accept in my conscious mind. I needed, with a need that developed toward intensity, to understand clearly the bases, within myself, of this conflict.

Each special line of interest on which the human mind goes out to make its discoveries in the world comes eventually to expression in its own particular type of phrasing, a kind of crystallization of language into form with particular meanings—a terminology. I had pondered deeply in several of these lines of interest and revelation—Theosophy, Christian Science, Spiritism, physiology, psychology, and other sciences—in search of a meaning, and in each of them I had caught glimpses of a clear light which lay behind them all, a light with which, in spite of all my work and honest effort, I had not succeeded in adequately identifying myself.

Yet in the long process of the years, which was really a rapid progress, I had gathered out of study and experience an impressionistic but true knowledge of the reality of that glimpsed basic light. I conceived and knew it as a vital source. And I also had an inner conviction that the identification of myself with that light was the key to the health and fulfillment that I had not yet achieved, but sought with a kind of spiritual intensity.

I know now that within each human being there exists a core or seed of individual compulsion and necessity. This is the matrix—the reason and the purpose—of the life. It is what we refer to, understandingly or not, when we use the word "soul." The pattern that is hidden in this seed must be fulfilled and cannot be denied; it is the meaning of the individual's existence as a participant in the cosmic process. Many people become so encrusted by the impedimenta of the world which is "too much with us" that they miss the meaning of their own existence and wear out their faculties of expression

---

* In Eileen J. Garrett (1939). *My Life as the Search for the Meaning of Mediumship*. New York: Oquaga Press.

in many purposes alien to their natures. They really never know, through all the years, how or why they *are* alive—or that they are alive within themselves. Such people live and move mainly in the fogs of the mass-consciousness, and never achieve self-realization until just before (if they are fortunate) or after death.

But during the years of life, the inner pattern will continuously exert its pressure on consciousness. When the strain between a man's two lives—inner and outer, basic and superficial—reaches too great a tension, illness, mental distress, or some other type of difficulty develops. The outer structure of activity and achievement is shattered, or arrested for a time at least, and consciousness is given an opportunity, perforce, to perceive and contemplate the true inner quality of the individual's uniqueness.

I had come through several such periods of enforced contemplation. In my own case, I feel that the lessons were drastic, not because the pattern of my life was "advanced" or superior to many other life-patterns, but because, under all outer activities, I was actually trying to find and understand the secret spring and aim of my existence. My consciousness was thus partially "conditioned" and ready to catch the impulses from my soul.

As one illness succeeded another through the years, and as my supersensory work became more significant and factual—through simple accumulation, if there had been nothing more—I finally reached a climax of inner distress that was compounded of physical insufficiency and a sense of utter psychological confusion. Looking at myself as calmly and objectively as possible, I realized that at the base of my nature there lay a fundamental demand for health—but more important, for clearer understanding.

In this situation my first gleam of clarification came in the idea that I must heal *myself,* physically and psychologically. "Physician, heal thyself." No one else could possibly know me as well as I knew myself. And from that idea I caught my first clue to the way out of my difficulties: I realized that I did not know my fundamental self at all. There were whole regions of my personality that were completely mysterious to me. Illness and lack of clear mental vision were conditions alien to the inner purposes of my life, I knew; yet I did not know what were the *positive* inner purposes of my life.

As a base to stand on, a foothold, I made to myself, and accepted, a confession of confusion. Presently, looking about for the direction in which I should move forward from this base, I perceived that I must rid my consciousness of all the elements that had come together to create the confusion—I must clear up my entire psychic field. I understood then, as I had not understood before, that both my mind and my emotions were congested by my quasi-faith in the ideas of ancient philosophies and modern sciences, and that terminologies constituted one of the factors of my *malaise*—quite literally, I was sick of terminologies, the vague preciseness of which reflected other men's perceptions, not my own.

So, to the best of my ability, I washed my consciousness clean of all the past. When I felt that this clearing of the field had been adequately accomplished, I held my consciousness still, poised and free of all content, and watched to see what indication, if any, would emerge into that area now devoid of forms.

What emerged was a sense of myself. It came very gently, without force, and I had to look at it steadily to be sure it was not evoked by some subtle inner volition or secret wish. But as I contemplated it, I came to know that it was a response to the deep need of my life, and that it had arisen from the center of my nature into the prepared bareness of my conscious mind. I had long been familiar with the process in which a symbol or an impression appears in one's consciousness, and in which one *knows* when one has caught the correct significance of such an appearance. I now knew, not merely mentally, but with every faculty of my personality, that my road to health and fullness of life—physical, emotional, mental, and spiritual—depended upon my deeper comprehension of myself.

From many people and books, I had received a great deal of advice; answers to questions and suggestions for methods of work. These had all been partial and diffuse, leading me outward into many fields of interest and experience; but actually they had all contributed to my final confusion and distress. Now I began to feel a strange new fusion or unity within myself, a singleness of purpose that had to do with nothing less than life—my individual life and an infinitely greater life in which I had my part to play, and in which my health and efficiency were of very real, I might almost say cosmic, importance.

This impression of my close alliance with cosmic importance was in no sense an expansion, but only a simplification, of my own personal importance. It was a new impressionistic conception of relationships. It contained no element of inflation of any kind, but consisted, rather, in a profound realization of my responsibility for the full expression of my life-potentials, and in a secondary or responsive feeling of joy in the discovery of the straight and simple way by which this responsibility was to be fulfilled.

On the basis of these clear and fundamental realizations, I established a new regimen of living. For six months I spent some part of each day in letting the fantasy of the subconscious have its play. In the evenings I went to bed at five o'clock, and remained in a lightly meditative state, without focusing my consciousness on any practical or productive themes, and with the door of my mind held open to perceive any inner impulse or activity sufficiently vital and significant to impress itself upon my ready awareness.

Day and night, during this time, I kept paper and pencil with me always. And sometimes the pencil in my hand would move, I knew not why, and would mark upon the paper the malformed or formless hieroglyph of some incomprehensible reflex. Such marks were like the strokes of the beginning of automatic writing, the early attempts of an inner impulse to express itself in form, free from the supervising purposes of the conscious mind. Like the early efforts of a young child to write with pen and ink, they lacked sequence and significant form, and proved only that somewhere deep within the sum of my psychological self there moved energies the potencies of which had never yet been realized or expressed.

Were these embryo potencies, these potentials, realizable or expressible under any circumstances whatever? For a time I did not know. As the only result of their activity I had accumulated a mass of pictorial dross—straight lines, curved lines, an occasional circle, square, triangle, or cross, drawn awry, a possible numeral, a suggestion of a face, a bird, or a flower—lines that intimated forms to the inquiring intelligence, but were no forms in fact.

Nevertheless, I was able to gather an impression of progression in the process. This was not the "doodling" that every normal person is supposed to practice during conversations over the telephone. There was present no sensory or critical supervision of the lines set down, no going over and over a figure to perfect its symmetry and blacken its outline. Any attempt to translate these marks into oral expression would have resulted in sound and fury of the crudest kind—screams and groans and grunts. They were the embryos of forms not yet developed. Yet I felt that they were mine, were me. I did not understand them—but I did not understand myself. Their vagueness reflected my own egotistic instability.

I am now sure that my impression of a progression occurring in these automatic pencil marks upon paper was correct, for there developed a period or stage in which, both within my inner vision and on paper, there began to appear what was to become a long series of symbols, inchoate too, but beginning to struggle into form. I was like one who unearths an ancient lost city. Having dug down through layers of late surface deposits, I was at last coming upon remnants of the past which had significance of their own, however unilluminating and intrinsically valueless they might be.

Later still, I began to see suggestions of flowers and animals—not complete and perfect forms, but sections that were often indicative and sometimes unmistakably suggestive. There were outlandish beasts and birds and flowers, like nothing that I had ever seen in real life, in natural histories, or in art. They *might* have burgeoned briefly in the age of the great reptiles, but I had no reason to suppose that they ever had. They were symbols, pure and simple; but the meaning of their appearance, as they came and went upon the inner screen of my perception, was completely unknown to me. My conscious mind was sure that no such creatures had ever lived on this or any other planet—yet there they were, and I was not imagining them. It was not in the levels of imagination that they appeared, but out of deep and shadowy psychological levels that have not yet been named.

Before long I began to *feel* their significances. And in that experience I found again how the human mind learns from and through the far more ancient emotions. What I felt was power, a tremendous force of life itself that animated these gross and turgid symbols that I saw. The colors of flowers expressed a savage fury, birds were taloned and multi-winged, beasts were massive congestions of ravenous vital energy. Life had somehow clotted frantically into forms, of which these amorphous shapes that I perceived were unreliable reproductions made in deep, dark realms—deeper than any dream.

They were sometimes terrifying, often repulsive. Under the thrusting aggressive energy, which was my main impression of their innate quality, I would sometimes grow psychically weary and fall into sleep.

Out of such sleep I always waked refreshed—not simply as we are all refreshed by normal sleep, but vitally renewed, as though in some secret cave of my being a new spring of energy had been tapped, enabling me to continue and proceed in these deep investigations in which I was engaged. This seemed strange to me, even while I recognized the fact, for my sleep was not of that placid kind which we commonly think of as normal. The great dynamic beasts and vegetable growths occupied my subconscious constantly. The sweep of vital energy that raged through them would rise in a swift emotional spiral of aversion or fear, and I would suddenly wake, distressed and gasping, to the calm realities of the world of the conscious. Yet in each renewal of such uprushes from the depths I suffered a less overwhelming distress, and I gradually came to realize that the subconscious was able to deal with these chimerical forms and conditions as my conscious modern mind was not.

In a certain sense, such waking was an escape *from* the subconscious, as my going to sleep was an escape *into* it. In the process as a whole, I was undoubtedly achieving a unity of consciousness within myself. And not only that: I was also widening, on a vast scale, my consciousness-relationships in supersensory areas of the space-time field.

I believe that I reached down, deep into the racial past, to times and conditions with which we have lost all rational contact. It was not a strange world to the whole psyche, however, because (as I learned by deliberate experiment) the subconscious traveled far in those subliminal regions, stirring up awareness *only when it became necessary* (as it seemed) for awareness to perceive—perceive, experience, and accept—some new symbolic aggression of color, some wilder embodiment of crashing force. I came to feel, as this process of interplay went on, that I was achieving within myself brand-new foundations of health, capability, and consequent assurance, for the living of a life which, in one sense, was to be *my* life, but which, in another sense, was to transcend my individuality and operate on impersonal levels that might be thought of as universalistic—though limited, of course, to the fields of our practical human existence.

In the end—the end of confusion, at least, because the chaos of symbols began to clarify—I knew that I had come close to my primeval beginnings. For a time I was immersed in a great darkness whose quality was wholly negative. It was a state of being that lay deeper than evil. It was utter ignorance, nescience, and formless. But it was potent—impressively so, and irksome. It was the darkness of a primeval chaos, before light and the revelations of light ...

I was penetrating here at a depth which I can now think of only as spiritual. There was nothing moralistic about the phase, either good or evil; but I was perceiving, symbolically, the dark bases in myself, out of which man's moral concepts have emerged. I had no moral sense or thought, at this stage, but I was myself the great darkness, the depths of that nescience were contained in me. I had a clear, free, strong sense of myself, however, that penetrated the utter identity of myself and the darkness. I understood the significance of the psyche at its base—the core of nature in all things—which at once unites me to and separates me from the universal. At times I suffered agonized realizations of exclusion, limitation, and loneliness too deep for explanation; at other times I seethed with the power that was in me—I was a master, a creator, a conqueror in my own field, and that field was extensive. My three selves were fused together in a state of unity beyond analysis or definition.

Waking from such dreams or day-dreams, I was intensely conscious of my physical body. Consciousness seemed to be centered in my solar plexus, but I was inwardly aware of all the world as extending outward from that center. The entire pelvic region would ache, as from tension, yet there was no tension; my diaphragm would be painful with rigidity, yet there was no rigidity anywhere in my body. It seemed as though consciousness itself were searching my organism with a harsh, penetrative hand and drawing into itself the essence of all that it touched.

When this searching process was completed, consciousness, thus vitalized from every secret source of myself, moved out into the infinite. And I knew within myself, as all this developed, that my ego—the seeded core of my individual life—was unified, integrated within itself, and was satisfied and ready for experience in the whole broad field of its affinities.

There followed a series of experiences which seemed to occur in an entirely different cosmic dimension. The symbols which I have described were all of the earth earthy—primal energy massed into forms whose quality was a persistent aggressiveness. They were dynamic force warring against itself—separated parts seeking wildly to be reunited with the whole to which they belonged. Without intention or purpose, they were vicious in their very nature, driven by the inner pains of their restrictive individualization. But I came now to a fresh phase of revelation. Dynamism still throbbed and soared and struggled in this new field, but the symbols were of a different character. Broken suns and moons and stars and streams of light-energy wove broken arcs of movement through the dimensions of space which were everywhere. They glowed and flashed and collided within me, and at the same time I floated among them, as if upheld upon the surface of a water, far from the center of myself.

At the base of all these silent but stupendous flashings there was blood. I bled. I *felt* myself bleeding, in single drops that gathered and swelled and burst; and the burst fragments, bursting again, were scattered abroad in the shards of moving stars and bright energies.

There were times when I felt the process acutely. I felt myself bleed inwardly, in the heart, in the kidneys, in the liver, in the lungs, and I *saw* these exudations of myself gather, accumulate, enlarge, and break; and I *felt* them break, with pain, into fragmentary star shapes that moved within me—for I was dimensionless and everywhere, even while I realized my own organic structure and the unity that existed between my organs and these symbols of infinity.

There were other phases in this whole chimerical experience the general nature of which I have tried to intimate. By the end of six months I knew that I had traveled far in what, for most people, is forbidden territory. Actually, it is not forbidden territory; but to enter into it one must have an unmistakable foundation in one's own centralized and critical psyche. One must always know subjectively, at the very core of one's life, that in such experiences one is recapitulating the deepest qualities inherent in one's being; and that while the phases of the recapitulation represent actual ingredients in one's psychological make-up, they are symbolic representations, *and therefore objective*, exhibited for interpretation by the individualized mind. I do not recommend such experiments as my own. No two such experiences could possibly be alike, or even similar, probably. I was led into the undertaking by pressures of vital necessity that moved within me—pressures which (perhaps fortunately) most people do not feel acutely.

At any rate, in my own case, by the end of six months, I had an inner feeling of repletion from all that had entered into my awareness in extraordinary ways—or at least from extraordinary depths. For six months I had lived very largely at nonsensory levels. And I knew within myself that the whole experience would be valueless and wasted unless I could translate it into other forms that would be acceptable—in the sense of being understandable—in the conscious areas of my mind. All translation, all explanation, is a process of *informing*, or creating significant form in consciousness. I had experienced a plethora of forms that were significant in themselves; but unless I could transpose them into other forms that would be directly significant for me, I should find that, instead of clarifying my original confusion, I had simply added further complications to it.

At this stage my only key to progress was emotion, feeling. I had to bring the elements of my experience into order, and as a basis for doing so I had a host of emotional memories from the episodes themselves—if one may call them episodes.

This transformation of swiftly moving, bizarre, and broken symbols into any system of conscious comprehension was not in itself a simple undertaking. Actually, it had to work itself out; I could not bring the inner meanings up into consciousness by any sort of compulsion. A new level of consciousness was now to take up the work from the stage which had already been accomplished; and between this new level of consciousness and the deep subconscious which had been working so furiously, so to say, the only apparent bridges were memory and emotion. But there was also the will. The clairvoyant symbols that I had known from my earliest memories moved to help me, but it was finally through the tenacity of the will—sustaining patience and holding in arrest all responses to remembered symbols and emotions which had occurred in the chaotic fluid flight, until they gave up their secrets—that the levels of the experience became clarified into comprehensible strata.

I came in time to understand that the yew tree represented my own private structure, myself. It had appeared only in the second phases of the subconscious revelation. But the symbols of furious energy which had constituted the first phase had risen out of depths that were in fact more ancient and primeval than my own individuality had ever known. Yet somehow—though exactly how I could not define—a line of contact went back from my own beginnings into that past. I knew that out of that era that predated the individualization of my own consciousness I had been evolved—had become "ensouled," or at least embodied, and thus a representative and conveyor of the blood. In the era of the blood, I reviewed my *hereditary* past. The serpent of separateness was then in me, and I was in him; but neither of us was confined and separated in fact, for our outer relationships extended far into time and space, and we were allied to the basic nature of the planets and the stars.

Here in the blood I had the symbol of my heritage; and by virtue of that heritage I had become differentiated in the racial mass consciousness and somehow alienated from the levels of life in which primal energies flowed in unembodied power and freedom. I had passed through the crucible of the spirit, out of which all identities are fashioned into form.

It was a long process of fusion between the subconscious and the conscious. Many of the symbols remembered and felt could not find a place in the simplicity of this final pattern. But I emerged with the conviction, tested by repeated probings, comparisons, and questionings, that I had actually surveyed the basic content of my subconscious. I had caught a direct and potent sense of the incomprehensible primavera, of the racial mass, of my individualization and direct heritage. While the experience was of a kind that could never be adequately diagrammed objectively, I understood clearly in my own consciousness (though never clearly enough) how I had come into existence out of the timeless past, in a process of natural evolution, and that I was destined to do my share in carrying the process forward into the endless future.

I am now convinced that the life process is one in which primal energy is finding a progressive way back, through form, to a unity which has been disturbed but can never be broken. The key to the process is consciousness—the release of consciousness from restrictive limitation in and by form. The consciousness of all created things is potentially capable of transcending the limits of the forms which are its instruments, and of finding immensely wider fields of relationship and activity than these seem to impose. This is the *way* of consciousness—of life. It is because this is so that, in the material world, higher kingdoms in nature consume the substance of the lower kingdoms; and it is because this is so that the aspirations of mankind transcend men's comprehension, while man's innate capacities transcend all the data of the world of sense.

Actually, we are free of the restrictions of automatism that bind the mineral and vegetable kingdoms, yet the human consciousness clings to whole series of automatic activities, not all of which are inescapable. We are also potentially free of the self-reference of instinct which so inevitably binds the animal kingdom, yet consciousness clings tenaciously to the level of self-interested thought and action.

But these facts mark our alliance with the past, not with the future. As a matter of fact, the human consciousness is rapidly freeing itself from the restrictions of form. Having lifted substance into the sky, and having circumvented the natural law of gravity —thus conquering the last of the four ancient elements of earth, water, fire, and air—man's next step to freedom would seem to be possible only in the areas of consciousness. Presently, in the infinities of space-time, man may travel in consciousness wherever he will—if he will.

In the long and disturbing process of penetrating the subconscious, I followed a line of action which was, for me—in spite of its difficulties—a line of least resistance, for it was established in the imperative inner need of my being. I have no reason to suppose that any other person could or would experience a similar sequence of episodes. My earliest years had been full of a natural fantasy. I lived largely—and most happily—in a symbolic world.

I was made that way. When I later went deep into the subconscious, it was probably inevitable that my self-realization should be clarified by symbolic means.

There were some factors of that experience, however, that I have not yet completely clarified in my conscious mind. For instance, I have made but a single passing reference to the serpent. Actually, in the whole process which I have described, the serpent was a most important symbol. As I perceived it, it was an emblem of struggle, conflict, and distress. I know now that out of struggle, conflict, and distress wisdom develops; yet I have no sure sense within myself that the serpent of wisdom has come to dwell with me.

Lying still in contemplation, I sometimes see the conflicts of my early years. They appear, symbolically, as thongs interlaced, like a clot of tiny serpents writhing within and around my respiratory channels. I have also seen other organs of the body related to symbols, the liver always taking its place as the sun, while the heart appeared in the placid character of the moon. I have seen certain muscles of the body as related to the animal world. The phase of blood which I have described—rivers of blood—became as the depths of the ocean bed filled with a million creatures. Pain and bodily conflict show themselves, now, in symbols, always before an illness. Repeatedly through the years an illness emanating from the liver has been shown as the symbolic Sun, spotted or colored a smoky yellow ...

The symbolism of my youth and the symbolism of my maturity are both parts of myself—media for my understanding; and though I have a sense of different phases in the development of the process as a whole, I know that, for me, symbolism is a means of revelation. In the present times I am often confronted by a symbol whose structure is suggestive of a spearhead. It dances before me when I am to be approached to start some new endeavor. If it flattens out and ceases to be active, the project is potential only, and will not be worked out. I have seen this symbol days, and even weeks, before the project it represented became known to me. Star symbols still often convey a confusion of mind. When I am over-tired, I see them frequently; but they are also, at other times, fine avenues of light in which I see the beginnings of many things take shape. In these star-shaped symbols, if the lines of light break and burst and do not again come together, I know that I need a change of activity and relaxation ... There are many other symbols in my experience, some of which I have never verified in active reality—laurel leaves, for instance. When I have seen them for myself, they have carried an urgency to some vigorous achievement. Sometimes they turn into sharp, spear-like shapes over the heads of other people, and then I know that *they* are in a process of achievement for themselves. The smell of laurel—the tasted odor—means healing, fulfillment, development; but this I know only from my inner knowing, not from actual experiment or use.

In a certain sense, these symbols—all symbols—are abstractions. To say this does not rob them of reality, however. They are stimuli which appear to awareness out of one's psychic being, just as an object or a sound in the physical world may affect awareness through the sense of sight or hearing. In like manner, they are not merely sporadic occurrences, but are directly related to real events in the life of the world. Behind the perception of a symbol, as behind the hearing of a sound, there lies the important process of understanding what the received impression means. Such interpretations of perceived symbols, whether these be physical or psychic, constitute the sum and quality of our human lives.

XI
Trance and the Controls

THERE ARE NUMEROUS THEORIES which have undertaken to explain and account for the occurrence which is known as "trance," but it still remains mysterious. Sleep-walking, ordinary dreaming, certain hypnotic states, catalepsy, stupor, and so on are all loosely referred to as trance states. But such states, for the most part, are alien to the interest of this book; what I wish to speak of is, of course, the condition that is known as "mediumistic trance."

Trance of this type is historically ancient, and from time immemorial has been called "possession." "Possession" was formerly associated with the idea of evil; one was "possessed of devils"; but it is significant that psychological study and analysis, down the ages, have clarified our understanding of most of these "evil" affections, so that today the idea of possession applies principally to the trance state, and the trance state has been cleared of these evil connotations. Mediumistic trance still suffers faintly from some associated practices of charlatanism and "magic," but true trance has adequately justified itself as an actual condition occurring in human psychology, and is scientifically classified and recognized. In these times, trance possession generally connotes the use of a "sensitive's" personality, by some disembodied intelligence, for communication with humanity from some non-human area of consciousness.

Though trance is thus recognized, it is not understood. The scientists are not ready to agree among themselves concerning just what occurs in the psyche of the individual who enters into trance. There are two principal schools of thought on the subject. One school emphasizes the "dissociation" theory, which holds that the consciousness of the sensitive becomes concentrated on some particular idea or state of being so that the normal activities of many of his nerve-groups are inhibited, and that he speaks or writes out of his own knowledge and experience, though he may have no conscious awareness of the material which he thus brings to expression.

This theory seemed, for a time, to promise further light on the mysterious nature of trance. But every theory is a challenge to the world to prove it either right or wrong, and if it is not too obviously unsound, the new theory becomes the basis for just such experimental tests. The "dissociation" theory thus became the basis for new tests, and the general result of these was that the theory of "possession," which seemed to be about to be discarded, was instead revived, since the results of the experiments revealed considerable data which the theory of dissociation did not seem adequately to account for.

Very briefly and broadly stated, the dissociation theory inevitably rests upon the supposition that in trance the sensitive reveals what he has some-how—however unconsciously—known or experienced. But certain experiments, conducted principally by the Society for Psychical Research, and largely with the American medium, Mrs. Piper, produced communicated material of which (it was accepted) the sensitive could not conceivably have had any personal knowledge. So the ancient theory of possession was revived.

At this point of indetermination, clairvoyance enters into the situation, complicating it further. Many of the "dissociationists" do not accept telepathy or clairvoyance as such, any more than they accept the idea of possession by disembodied "controls." Yet to some of them, telepathy or clairvoyance seems to suggest a possible further support for the dissociation theory.

As I have indicated in the chapter on consciousness, clairvoyance is not a person's reading of some other person's mind, but is the nonsensory perception of persons, conditions, and events which exist and occur in time and space, distant from the perceiver. Clairvoyance is a direct and conscious activity of the perceiver—even though he may not know how it "works"—while in the mediumistic trance the sensitive is unconscious and does not know what he is transmitting. Whether or not the capacities by means of which clairvoyance occurs operate also in some mysterious way in the trance state, is still a shadowy hypothetical question. It should be noted that, technically, clairvoyance is the power of perceiving and knowing by means in which neither the ordinary processes of sensory perception operate, nor any super-normal communication with other intelligences, incarnate or discarnate, occurs. It is a process of direct, nonsensory, conscious knowing. The process by which communication occurs through trance would not seem, therefore, to include the clairvoyant faculty, at least in the sense in which we now understand clairvoyance.

With this partial failure of the dissociation theory to account for the controls who are supposed to manifest through the trance of a sensitive, there developed an experimental technique of "cross-correspondences" in communicated material. Mrs. Piper's controls were also communicating through other sensitives, and it was thought that if, in the automatic writings or trance communications of one of these people, there could be found incomplete and incomprehensible fragments of statement which could be made intelligible when associated with similar fragmentary statements in the writings or communications of another of these people, a strong case might be built up for the factual reality of a third intelligence as the originator of the whole passage thus scattered. A considerable measure of success was achieved in this work. But it hardly amounted to any direct proof, and though it refuted, in some measure, the dissociation theory, it left the whole question of the nature of trance communication still mysterious, and very much where it was before the dissociation theory was proposed.

Nevertheless, many competent observers in the field of psychic phenomena still hold that dissociation is the key. They suggest that dissociated fragments of a sensitive's personality may become synthetized into a kind of second personality, capable at times of assuming control of the organs of expression, and able also to control certain clairvoyant or telepathic faculties of the organism.

The condition which is known as mediumistic trance is, therefore, not understood or defined.

One may suppose that the person most intimately interested in the actual process which occurs in mediumistic trance is the medium or sensitive who submits to the trance condition. Yet he is the person most definitely debarred from helping our understanding toward a solution of the mystery, because during the period of trance he is unconscious—unaware of himself, of his environment, and of the material which is being communicated through him. On his return to "normal" he is often intensely interested, even surprised, in the material that has been revealed. Entering into the trance state, he does not know what control may use his organism, or what may be expressed through it.

For the sensitive who is naturally of an inquiring disposition, this situation is in a certain sense baffling; and whenever a new control speaks or writes through his trance, he is naturally led to wonder what may have happened to *him*, that this fresh phenomenon should have occurred.

I have not personally attempted to penetrate these mysteries in recent years, however, for I learned the lesson of acceptance. In relation to an activity in which one surrenders up one's will, volitions, and consciousness, the lesson of acceptance is not easy to learn; but observing both the inadequacies and the high values of the communicated material, I have found much of both of them alien to my own conscious thought and expression, and I have given over my early sense of responsibility for the manifestations of the trance state. This has been much easier for me to do since all of my controls have been consistently kind, considerate, wise, and serviceable to those who came to them for help.

Is the mediumistic trance a condition of possession? I cannot say. I have raised this very question in the past and have been censured for doing so. The certainty that the controls are disembodied though individualized intelligences, operating from another plane of consciousness than ours, is based on the controls' own assertion that this is so, as well as on the fact that information, advice, healing, and teaching of a high order have been communicated through the trance of sensitives. This communicated material, in voluminous measure, has been alien to, and superior to, the normal knowledge and capacity of any of the sensitives through whose trance it has come.

To anyone who is capable of telepathic and clairvoyant activities, capable also of projection and pre-cognition, the revelations which occur in trance constitute a baffling type of impasse. To surrender up, temporarily, all of the phases of consciousness in which these capacities, and the awareness of them, inhere, and to become the means, through this surrender, for communications from the known dead, for instance, places one at a peculiar point of self-consciousness. Inevitably, at first, one wishes deeply to discover and know the process by which the "unconscious" revelation has occurred. But one does not discover the "how" of it, and eventually, in the name of service, one simply accepts the facts as they are. One submits to the "higher intelligence," whether this be an objective consciousness or some factor, or combination of factors, of one's own personality.

Personally, I have no determinations to announce concerning the nature and identity of the controls that communicate through my trance. Regardless of all our questioning and lack of understanding, they are what they are. This I accept. It is in no spirit of disloyalty, therefore, that I say, quite frankly, that I have the highest hopes for the evolutionary development of the human consciousness and human faculties; and if, some day, it should be revealed that the controls are factors of my own psychic being, I should experience neither satisfaction nor regret, but should continue to make my surrenders for the service of humanity, just the same as now.

In passing, I wish to note three of the main divisions of faculty which correspond to our three main divisions of consciousness. These are anesthesia (subconscious), aesthesia (conscious), and hyper-aesthesia (superconscious). The word "aesthesia" comes from two Greek words meaning "sensation," plus "to perceive"—hence, sensory perception and sensation. Anesthesia is a condition in which there is an absence of perception and sensation—the sub-aware areas of consciousness. And hyperesthesia? Here again we face the whole problem of those higher capacities of the human consciousness which transcend perception, sensation, memory, imagination, and reason; and from this point, we may look forward with faith and aspiration to the future development of the nameless potentialities of the human psyche.

As additional evidence pointing to the future development of the human consciousness, I should like to quote from Professor Rhine's conclusions based on his long and careful experimentation in clairvoyance at Duke University.*

> We posed the question (What is the human mind?) as still the most fundamental in modern psychology, if not in life itself. It seemed possible to find a new approach to this question by re-examining and investigating an ancient and accepted doctrine of our science—the belief that nothing can enter the mind except through the gateways of the recognized senses. This psychological dogma had become, we pointed out, an old and almost undisputed frontier of the mind, one that has had much to do with shaping the general view of its nature which we hold today.
>
> The research itself represents a critical testing of this dogma of the inviolability of the mind's sensory frontier. If we could find any extra-sensory avenue to knowledge, not only would that concept cease to be the circumscribing law of mind it was once considered, but a new frontier, a further horizon would be established.
>
> That new frontier has now been established unless all of us who have been exploring it by years of testing and many hundreds of thousands of trials have been completely and continually self-deluded or incompetent, not only at the Duke laboratory but elsewhere as well. Either delusion is the explanation of our results or else we have found proof that the mind of man does indeed have an extra-sensory way of perceiving, and hence, whether we like it or not, the old frontier must go the way of Newtonian mechanics in the light of relativity.

Uvani was the first control who used my trance for communication. Over a period of several years, he gave repeated evidence of the survival of human life beyond death, and transmitted messages of the most personal nature between people living on this earth and their known "dead" in the conditions of the "beyond."

Uvani has given a picture of himself on earth as "an insolent, intolerant Arab, taking his pleasures regardless of any who came his way." But in all of his communications, he has appeared most gentle, kind, and meticulously considerate. The change in his nature has occurred, he says, since his death. On earth he was Yusuf ben Hafik ben Ali, a member of a noble merchant family of Basrah, connected principally with the export of fruit.

---

* In J. B. Rhine (1937). *New Frontiers of the Mind.* New York: Farrar & Rinehart.

He lived something more than a century ago, and at the time of his death he was about forty-eight years of age. He was killed while fighting against the Turks. The name "Uvani," which he has assumed, means "The Son of Happiness."

Abdul Latif (Abd-ul-Latif), who later came to use my trance as a means of communication, is said to have been a Persian. Born in Baghdad in the twelfth century, he died in the thirteenth, at the age of sixty-nine. He was a physician and astronomer who traveled extensively, and he was connected with the court of Saladin in the time of the Crusades. Baron Sylvestre de Lacy collected and transcribed the numerous references to Abdul Latif in Arabic literature, and in the Bodleian Library, at Oxford, there is a book written by Abdul Latif himself, concerning which Mr. R. H. Saunders[*] has written as follows:

> It is known as *Al Mokhtasir, The Compendium.* It is on parchment six and one-half inches wide and nine and three-quarter inches high, and consists of one hundred and thirty-three pages written in the beautiful Arabic characters. It is yellow with the age of some seven centuries, but the writing is clear, with not a single alteration or correction, and is in Abdul Latif's own handwriting. It treats of his travels in Egypt, with observations on its conditions in A.D. 1200, and is the mine in which historians for centuries have delved for information of that period.

I am giving these brief notations on the histories of two of my principal controls because in the past I have raised the question of their reality as personalities who have spoken through my trance. As a matter of fact, I have no wish to impugn their integrity or their reputation, and the question is again dealt with here because people who, in the past, have known of my uncertainty on the point, still write to me, asking if I have come to a conclusion.

I have not arrived at any new or definite determination. But it must be understood that, in a certain sense, I consider the problem a purely personal one. It is not at all based on any wish to deny or refute Uvani and Abdul Latif, but rather arises out of my sincere wish—as well as my private need—to discover the factual reality of the whole process by which the controls presumably communicate. I have a definite feeling that we are perhaps on the verge of further revelation on the whole subject of controlled communication, and I have an inner certainty that this new knowledge will be related to the nature and the capacities of the human consciousness.

---

* In R. H. Saunders (1927). *Health and Healing Through Spirit Agency.* London: Hutchinson.

In this chapter, therefore, I have decided to touch upon several points connected with the whole problem. I trust it will be understood that these points are offered simply as lights reflected from various facets of the question as a whole.

Anyone who has had a life-experience at all similar to my own will have been faced, from time to time, with problems of so subjective and vital a nature that it has been imperative they be solved within the individual's own consciousness, regardless of all specific teaching and any general consensus of opinion on the themes. Such persons receive knowledge and understanding from two sources—the general sensory field and certain nonsensory areas of intuitional experience. And in case of a failure of these two lines of effect readily to fuse and integrate with the present sum of the individual consciousness, at any particular time, there arises a problem the solution of which can develop only out of the nature of the problem itself.

In previous chapters I have given some account, partly factual and partly impressionistic, of my own life-experience, and it will perhaps be clear how all of that has led up to my present psychological need to achieve an understanding which I can myself inwardly accept, of the controls and their processes.

Up to the present moment, I have not been completely able, within myself, to accept the controls as separate intelligences. The hierarchy of every religion includes such beings, I know, and my faith in human survival beyond death might seem to be an adequate foundation for their acceptance. Yet at the same time, the whole appeal of religion and psychology is to the development of the *individual* human consciousness. The practical fact is that neither my faith nor my psychic experience has brought me into objective conscious contact with such entities as the controls, while our well-developed science, in spite of many attempts, has not found any means for differentiating them from my own individuality.

While modern psychology continues to pile up data concerning abnormal states of being, and begins to have its measure of success in the readjustment of *individual* cases, I am mainly concerned with human destiny as a whole. I have the feeling that, for most people, religion and immortality are like a promissory note; but I am deeply moved to discover the actual power and integrity behind the note's symbolic signature. If this signature is in fact a symbol of some level of my own being—a memento which some portion of my psyche presents to awareness—then I shall find the "controls" within myself, and I shall also be able to find means for further coordinating an apparent subjective and objective duality into a new unity *in my own consciousness.*

But if the controls are separate individualized entities, with means of knowing which I do not naturally and potentially possess, then my need is to be more useful than I am already—more useful to them.

It must not be supposed that I do not wish to *know*, to find the solution to this psychological problem. At the moment, however, that solution unquestionably escapes all the capacities of my apprehension. But I am especially anxious that this query in my own mind shall not create any conflict in the faith or understanding of other people. It is for further reality and clarity in the entire situation—a universally important situation, as I see it—that I continually seek.

My present state is not one of absolute conviction. Over long periods of time I tell myself that I could not possibly find, in my mind's knowledge alone, the answers that have come through me to the people seeking communication with the dead. I then have a childish, unquestioning faith that I have external help in this work, and like a child, I am deeply content that it should be so. In such times of deep peace and acceptance, I remain in a state of awe that I should be thus helped to help others, and I am filled with encouragement and optimism.

But there always comes a day when I ask myself by what right I deem the universe to be so arranged that I should be benignly attended by those whose life-patterns have already woven their way through this world. When these moments come, I am alone in that infinite loneliness of spirit in which awareness meets the self in areas of absolute being. My desire is then to be alone and to watch, unattended, the inner waves of light continue to shape my destiny.

Thus I behold my own condition and come face to face with myself—with inner patterns of will and initiative to achieve or create new strength. I see, as through a window, a long view down the roadway of my life, and I know how very fortunate I am to have had access to the place where I have experienced the radiation of the spirit into the world of matter.

It has been said that I am arrogant to question the validity of the controls. But in the light of my own understanding, I simply believe it has always been difficult for me to accept the fact that such beneficence should have been conferred upon me.

It has been pointed out that I tacitly concede too much to the finite human consciousness. But for myself I have had to believe that I found a way to that universal reservoir of being in which all events occur and are to be found—and within which is also to be found the key to the way of our own growth, to our brothers' growth, and indeed, to the evolution of all of life.

This also I have known: were I curtly to make up my mind about the ways and means in which consciousness operates, I should thus close the door to the present normal adventuring of my life, and to many meanings still to come. The growth of sensitivity is eternally progressive. I am continually becoming aware of new and unexpected channels for the exploration of consciousness. To be certain that one has reached an ultimate in truth is to endanger not only oneself, but truth also. To say "I know" would mark an acceptance, a conclusion which might close the door on the mystery of the light that continues to lead me to exploration and adventure. This problem of the nature of the controls is really the key to the field of my present pioneering.

When questioned about my attitude to them, the controls are always generous. They state and hold fast to their own reality; they refer to me as being "beloved" of them. And here are purity and greatness, since loving involves giving, and there is no giving that exceeds serving and creating for the beloved. I have always been aware of this truth. It has taught me the renunciation of pettiness and the glory of service.

To resolve my mind to a conclusion without further evidence, would, therefore, be to admit that I am finished with the adventure of the spirit. But I am not finished with the adventure—the adventure of life as a whole. When I am faced with the task of helping others, I seek those deeper levels of being out of which I have drawn compassionate help during the years—the depths beyond sleep into which I have gone and found unfailing wisdom and unselfishness, as well as constant reminders of my responsibilities. Therefore, I accept, with graciousness and good will, the controls whom I cannot explain or definitely understand.

Many people believe that the personality of the controls has been established, since they have themselves had experiences in which the controls have manifested to and through them. On the other hand, I have long since come to the belief that if the controls are splits in *my* personality, they have a right to use names for purposes of identification and clarity.

The statements of the controls do not always agree with my conscious personal opinion. If they make statements that seem to be very close to my own viewpoint, I say there is no difference between us. If a difference occurs, I am surprised and my problem is renewed; but in such cases I am not responsible, and so no conflict eventuates.

One cannot explain certain gifts or faculties, such as a good ear for music, a splendid singing voice, or some outstanding moral strength or weakness. They are there, parts of the natural make-up of the individual. Thus, the controls may be unidentified parts of myself, or—as many people prefer to think—they may be separate entities. In either case, what is most important is that the functions represented by the controls shall continue to create the patterns of constructive understanding—out of their own deep intuition or out of mine. All things draw their sustenance from the same infinite life and spirit. It is man's nature to be concerned with processes.

Moreover, if the controls are truly themselves, then they most surely understand that my questions and doubts are based on nothing but an imperative need to keep faith with life and myself—and with them, in reality, also.

My early failure to accept the controls at the unquestioning high level at which many people did and do accept them, received support, in a certain sense and measure, from the attitude of Hewat McKenzie, in whose integrity and judgment I had every confidence. I quote a paragraph from a former book* on this point:

> Hewat McKenzie was the only one of the leaders of the spiritualist movement who refused to take any pronouncement of a control personality as inevitably the word of some "Higher Power." He explained to me that, in his estimation, the possibilities of trance mediumship had been wasted and allowed to deteriorate, so that it now mainly functioned on emotional and sentimental levels. This was due to the fact that when the controls first appeared after a potential medium became entranced, no one regarded them as limited personalities who might themselves need help and training, in order to understand the highest use of their own position and functioning. He explained to me that a control personality is only an interpreter of what reaches him from other states of consciousness, and therefore he (the control personality) had to be taught how to make the purest use of his powers and to transmit only from the highest levels of truth.

I do not mean to intimate that Hewat McKenzie is in any way responsible for my own present lack of certainty. His attitude was entirely different from mine. But it was in this atmosphere of a deep desire to understand the actual *realities* of communication that I had much of my early training, and I am still endeavoring to understand them more clearly.

Later, Uvani, questioned by some of my more objective sitters concerning the process that he uses in communication, has stated, more than once, that he receives messages by means of visual impressions and that he must interpret the meaning of these images in order to project them through my mind. In one case, he explained how he got the impression of the name of a sitter's dead sister, Prudence.

Uvani explained that he first saw an upright column. He was not certain, at first, whether it was intended to form a P or an F. He then saw the image of a purse, and then knew the letter to be a P. He asked whether the purse meant anything to the sitter. On receiving a negative response, he sought further association of the meaning of the word "purse." Words such as "caution," "saving," and "prudence" came to him. Then, with a flash, he said, "something fell into place," and he knew that the name was "Prudence." He announced this as the name of the sitter's dead sister, and the inquirer admitted that this was so.

The manner in which the name of the sister was secured by Uvani while I was in the trance state is exactly the same as that in which I work in my waking, clairvoyant state. The symbols appear, they have to be interpreted, and the interpretation occurs through a "flash" or "click" in understanding, by means of which the perceiver *knows*.

During my last visit to Cannes, I suffered a continuing distress that involved the very depths of my life and spirit. It was the early spring of 1940, a long stretch of weeks of uncertainty and tension. Europe had been plunged into war, but thus far Hitler had attacked France only psychologically and by indirection. In the First World War I had spent many months of my life in war service in France, and I was now appalled that all the suffering, pain, and death that I had seen and known in those earlier years had won nothing definite—it all had to be endured again. I knew, as everyone knew, that France awaited the return of the holocaust, and a deep impersonal apprehension filled my mind. The forms to which we had accustomed ourselves after 1918 were again to be shattered, the world was again to be shaken to its foundations, and I was sensitively aware, day by day, of the impending disaster.

In this condition of spiritual distress I went often to a little thirteenth-century church—St. Cassian's which stood in a circle of oak trees, two or three miles outside the town, on a small hill. The property adjoined the air field, which had threatened its removal, but without success. In the little church, I found an atmosphere which matched my own deep mood—a silence and a sense of peace so pure and so sustained as to be almost unearthly. And here St. Cassian spoke to me, telling me that the present church had replaced an original fifth-century chapel of his, and that before that, the place had been the site of a pagan shrine. I was myself sensitively sure that sacrificial human blood had been spilled here, and there was a sinister legend of six female skeletons which had been found buried under the cypresses of the avenue. But I also became inwardly aware that the spot had not only been the scene of sacrifice; it had been a place of miracles as well.

At all times I believe profoundly in the creative power of faith, and in the present circumstances I felt what was almost a compulsive force bidding me to put my faith in pawn on behalf of my friends. It happened that at that time I had three friends for whom life was being drastically difficult. One was ill, one was having the strain of unprecedented financial losses, and one was facing a social crisis. I was deeply moved to aid them all, but could discover no way in which I could be practically useful.

So at last, under the pressure of the time and place, I asked St. Cassian for three miracles—that the disaster which threatened each of my friends might be solved and averted in right ways, and that their present distresses might be turned into joy. And as the weeks went by I had news from each of my three friends. The illness of one had been healed; the financial threat to the second had been relieved by the notice of an unexpected legacy; the danger had been definitely removed from the future of the third.

So I went again to the little church to thank St. Cassian for his three miracles. And in the timeless silence of the empty place he said to me, "You asked for three miracles. I ask for but one. Will you do it for me? I caused this shrine to be erected in order that the faith of men might be justified through the healing of their distresses. But that purpose has been forgotten. You know the power is here, do you not? Will you, then, restore this shrine to its original intention, for only in that way can it again fully justify its existence?"

"I am willing in spirit and gratitude," I said, "but the flesh … What can I do? I have neither money nor prestige sufficient …"

"You recognize the power, and you have the faith."

"Yes, I have," I acknowledged. "And I will do what you ask—somehow."

"It is well," he said. 'You can also show me a kindness. In the Tanneron, I have another little shrine. It is known as the Shrine of St. Cassian. Be good enough to go there and open the door—that is all, just open the door."

A few days later I drove out and found the little chapel, which was in a ruinous condition, and I opened the door, as I had been directed. As I did so, three bats flew out, and I knew, strangely but clearly, that the little building no longer held the spirit of holiness, but was consigned to a fate of utter ruin and disintegration.

Incidentally I may say that the Church of St. Cassian, at Cannes, still awaits rededication to its original mission. To do something about this is my uncompleted undertaking. I do not possess St. Cassian's facility in miracles; yet I am very sure within myself that when this war is ended, and France is recovering from her wounds, St. Cassian's at Cannes will become an important center for the manifestation of new faith and healing in the world …

I have said that St. Cassian spoke to me, telling me about the founding of his church and suggesting ways in which I might serve him. In telling of the experience to friends, I have been asked, "But how did he speak to you? Were you in trance?" I was not in trance. I heard him speak to me directly, as one person might hear another speaking distinctly in an adjoining room. It was an unusual experience for me, in the drowsy sunlit afternoon—an aural experience, direct and purely sensory.

Historically, St. Cassian belonged to the early Church of the fifth century. Born in Provence, as it is thought, he became celebrated as a recluse and was one of the first founders of monastic institutions in western Europe. It is said that his religious affinities were always with the East; he visited Egypt and dwelt for several years among the ascetics inhabiting the desert behind the banks of the Nile. He was ordained by Chrysostom in 403, at Constantinople.

Throughout my whole life I have been aware of the fact that everyone possesses a second body, so to say—a double. This double is not to be confused with the "surround" to which I have referred. The double is a distinct fact in Eastern and theosophical teaching, and as such it is said to be an energy-body, a magnetic area associated with the physical human corpus, an area in which the immaterial forces of the cosmos, the solar system, the planet, and one's more immediate environment are normally transformed into the life and being of the individual. Theosophists speak of this area as the etheric double or the astral body. I do not myself *know* the nature and constitution of the double, yet I have no valid objection to offer offer towards the theory. The "surround" I take to be a phase in the operation of the double.

I perceive the double which is associated with each human body, and I have discovered in my own experience some of the means by which it can be consciously used for the expansion of the individual life and consciousness.

The double is the medium of telepathic and clairvoyant projection. Projection consists in the transfer of the centralization of one's consciousness—the purposive concentration of one's attention and awareness—beyond the circle of one's purely individual capacities. It involves a readjustment from "normal" of all parts and faculties of one's life. The metabolism of the physical organism is altered. For me, projection "occurs" from a point in the chest, above the breasts, and is accompanied by a sense of "pull" at this point, by a fluttering sensation there, by a palpitation of the heart, and by an acceleration of the breathing. If the projection is continued for a considerable length of time, a slight sense of choking develops in the larynx, and I become aware of a "heady" sensation in the forebrain. I should perhaps make it quite clear that during the projection I am conscious, in a subsidiary way, of these effects as sensations.

What is it that is projected? I cannot give a scientific answer to this question. But I know, for myself, that projection is an event in the field of energies. The will, the non-sensory perceptive capacities, and the faculty of awareness are the most obvious factors involved. Focused in these, a large measure of the life-force is lifted out of its ordinary routine of operations. The forces of the energy-body or double are drawn upon in a heightened measure and are fused in the immediate purpose, which is at once subjective and objective to the projector.

In other words, under the command of the will, all of the energies of the personal life are temporarily intensively focused on some point of purpose that lies outside the "normal" relationships of the individual life. Or, again, all of the faculties of the individual life are fused in identification with a condition that is completely objective to the individual life and consciousness.

The limitations of time and space are transcended, and one perceives, is aware, knows—hears, sees, feels, participates in—the data of distant conditions and events. The process and the possible results of such projection have been described in the book, *Thoughts Through Space*, and in the "Newfoundland Experiment," in *My Life as a Search for the Meaning of Mediumship.*

To read a distant mind, to be present in consciousness at a distant event—such experiences transcend our conceptions of the operation field of the human mind. Yet they do occur; and what seems to me to be implicit in this fact is unmistakable evidence that the mind of man is capable of transcending the field which we now commonly conceive to be its field.

How far does this transcendence go? To what heights or depths of the universal life is it capable of reaching? In my opinion, nobody knows these spaceless and timeless measurements. All that we know of the capacity at all, however, has been achieved through the operations of the human mind itself. In every authentic case, such projection evidences the discovery, by the mind of man, of facts that exist in space-time beyond all possible reaches of the sensory capacities. Even these discovered facts are not always substantial, except in the sense that thoughts are things. We must sooner or later alter our conceptions of thought, awareness, and the human mind. And in doing so, where shall we discover the controls to stand?

As I sometimes conceive the problem, there is posited the alternative suggestion that the various controls, instead of being individualized entities existing on another plane of intelligence than ours, represent and indicate a development of psychic abilities that is normal to the consciousness of the sensitives through whom the controls presumably communicate.

Uvani, Abdul Latif, and many other controls have communicated through numerous others besides myself. In these voluminous communications, recorded over a considerable period of time, I believe there lies a valuable field for psychological study and evaluation, with the possible reward of a new illumination of vast importance to the whole process of man's understanding of himself.

I believe that possibly there is a discoverable sequence of development from the stage of one control to the next, with a corresponding shift in the nature of the communicated material, both of which might be found to have parallels in the lives of the sensitives. Even if such a suggested study did not prove this point, we should undoubtedly learn something scientifically factual about the psychological processes of communication and mediumship. It is unquestionably in the psychology of the human individual that the several capacities of sensitivity are developed, and this, of course, is the point of our most immediate and practical interest.

I am endeavoring to give, here, indications of the nature of my present problem, without forcing any conclusions. For me, the problem is utterly realistic and vitally important. The whole of my past experience and all of my intuitions of the future are focused on it. In the humbleness of simple honesty, therefore, let me suggest that, without wishing in the least to displace Uvani, I sometimes wonder if I have not myself developed into a phase of telepathic and clairvoyant capacity which approaches his capacity for finding the materials which he communicates. I feel that I may offer this suggestion without disloyalty and without doing violence to any reality. Fundamentally and quite impersonally, the suggestion points the possibility that man does not have to die in order to discover and reveal distant states of being—distant in either time or space, or both. For me, Uvani somehow subtly signifies the past.

And in the same subtle, impressionistic way, Abdul Latif signifies the future. Does this impression of a difference between them connote some inner intuition of my own potentialities for future development? It must be remembered that, for me, the problem is not only personal; it concerns the very nature of man, the whole meaning of human life. Abdul Latif is objective to my inner apprehension in a sense in which Uvani is not. In Abdul Latif I experience a sense of power which stirs my profound respect, in the manner in which we commonly respond to power with which we are not yet familiar.

I believe it may shed a summarizing light on this aspect of the subject if I quote briefly from Dr. C. G. Jung's Commentary on the Tai I Chin Hua Tsung Chih, in *The Secret of the Golden Flower*.

> ... I always worked with the temperamental conviction that in the last analysis there are no insoluble problems, and experience has so far justified me in that I have often seen individuals who simply outgrew a problem which had destroyed others. This "outgrowing," as I called it previously, revealed itself on further experience to be the raising of the level of consciousness. Some higher or wider interest arose on the person's horizon, and through this widening of his view, the insoluble problem lost its urgency. It was not solved logically in its own terms, but faded out in contrast to a new and stronger life-tendency. It was not repressed and made unconscious, but merely appeared in a different light, and so became different itself. What, on the lower level, had led to the wildest conflicts and to emotions full of panic, viewed from the higher level of the personality, now seemed like a storm in the valley seen from a high mountain top. This does not mean that the thunderstorm is robbed of its reality; it means

that, instead of being in it, one is now above it. But since, with respect to the psyche, we are both valley and mountain, it seems a vain illusion if one feels oneself to be above what is human. The individual certainly does feel the effect and is convulsed and tormented by it, yet at the same time he is aware of a higher consciousness which prevents him from being identical with the effect, a consciousness which takes the effect objectively, and can say, "I know that I suffer" ... Here and there it happened in my practice that a patient grew beyond the dark possibilities within himself, and the observation of the fact was an experience of foremost importance to me. In the meantime, I had learned to see that the greatest and most important problems of life are all fundamentally insoluble. They must be so, because they express the necessary polarity inherent in every self-regulating system. They can never be solved, but only outgrown. I therefore asked myself whether this possibility of outgrowing, or further psychic development, was not normal, while to remain caught in a conflict was something pathological. Everyone must possess that higher level, at least in embryonic form, and in favourable circumstances, must be able to develop the possibility ...

My purpose in citing Jung is to intimate my appreciation of the fact that though I have spoken of my mental and psychic problem as purely personal, it has at the same time broader relationships in the psychological field. I have repeatedly experienced the "outgrowing" referred to, and in various methods which I have described in this book and elsewhere, I have repeatedly experienced the raising of the level of my consciousness. By means of psychic exercises and experiences I have cured myself, to a great extent, in the various departments of my physical, emotional, and mental being; and I have made progress in the unification of what Jung calls the duality of the conscious and the unconscious, but which I am impelled to think of as a three-part unity—subconscious, conscious, and superconscious. I know that individual "psychic" problems are problems in our understanding of the racial psyche, variously conditioned, and of its relations to the universal consciousness as a whole.

Are, then, the so-called "controls" mysterious factors of my own psyche? I do not know.

I do know that, in spite of deep inner determinations of my own, my life has been basically patterned for me from sources which seem to exist outside myself, and in several cases the controls, consulted by my friends, have known that my own determinations would never eventuate. Once again, I was determined to break with the past, and make a new start in a fresh environment—possibly Australia. Nevertheless I continued to work in England. I decided to abandon my work as a trance-medium; yet Abdul Latif, when asked about that, laughed lightly and said, "This is just a phase in her development. She will not give it up." And for a time I didn't. Hewat McKenzie repeatedly warned me about how I must live—no smoking, no alcohol, a general abstemious control of all possible appetites; and I have said to him, in effect, "On the day when, for the sake of mediumship, I have to give up living in ways that are normal for me, that day I shall give up mediumship instead." Yet the abstemiousness has developed naturally and without strain, and the sensitiveness has not been lost ...

It may be of interest if I reproduce on the following pages a set of three comparative charts of a metabolism test, with their respective indications of (1) my normal state; (2) a first trance state—Uvani; and (3) a second trance state—Abdul Latif. These charts were made six or seven years ago, and they are not scientifically valuable, since they are extracts from an experimental study which was never completed. They do give indications of differences, however—even if only by suggestion—differences in the states of consciousness in which they were made. I reproduce them for their graphic value, and for whatever interest they may have as incidental indicators. (See the figures that follow this chapter.)

There are people in England, France, and elsewhere abroad, as well as in America, who have been interested to follow wherever my curiosity might lead me. These passages are an answer to their letters of inquiry. Many of them have asked me for what I am searching. I believe the real answer is: for a way to live in a state of the completest happiness possible, according to my nature. To achieve this, I have let the brain alone. I am not at all certain that the brain is the seat of the mind, as we have been taught to believe; possibly mind transfuses the whole body. I do not conceive of mind as made up of a vast number of ideas, memories, and reflections, put together by accident. I think of it as a highly trained and perceptive self, which activates, uses, and controls every organ of the body, their inner relationships, and the outer relations of the organism as a whole. Each single idea is carefully built up of parts, creating thought and action, which in turn affect the substance of our world. What the substance of our world is we do not know. We know only how it appears to us, according to our present state of mind. From instruction, we know many things about the world, and these scientific data we accept; but we are still in the dark concerning the essential attributes, the essence, the true nature of matter. We are still ignorant of what we ourselves *are,* and of our real relations to the universe.

All this being so, how could I undertake to explain happiness? Only those who have already experienced it would understand what I mean. Basically, happiness comes from giving. I do not mean simply giving the raw materials of the substantial world in the shape of possessions, but giving also—and freely—praise, service, love, sympathy; giving oneself to the natural scene, and giving sincere thankfulness to life for each day. I mean giving of the essence of one's being, a light in the eyes, the touch of a hand, sympathy in words; giving oneself to the magic of the moment, and to the elements; giving whether the way be hard or pleasant, but always giving what one has and is—giving life to life. Only this creates happiness and makes possible the adequate gratitude with which one receives whatever life brings to one in return.

This is a simple but basic philosophy. I have carried a dream of the world in my heart—the ultimate perfection and wholeness of man. To adopt "an attitude" toward that vision would be to mar it. Perfection cannot be achieved with ease, for ease is an interim between one task to be accomplished and the next. So I am primarily concerned with the methods of my own living; if these be right in the circumstances of the present, a million years hence my dream of ultimate perfection will still be authentic, creative, and true.

I have been asked what *I* think is the truth by which one should live. I have given my answer above—to be at one with the whole. The world is still seeking a concept of truth, as were the Greeks and those who came before them. Truth, so far as I am personally concerned, is the principle on which I express the experience and the energies of my life. Each man's own heart must lead him to perceive *his* truth. Each life has its own reason. But for man, true idealism and practical materialism cannot be separated, any more than spirit and body can be divided in life. I am content to leave dogma to the dogmatists; for myself, I retain the responsible philosophy of unity with the Absolute.

I conceive of individuality as being preserved forever within the highest principles of order. I conceive of the body as being the vessel of the mind. My reflections, sensations, and even my actions, I believe, are governed from the outer mind, the universal mind.

To conceive thus, then, is to concede that the controls, being parts of that eternal stimulus, may very well be what they claim to be. Indeed, at this point in my development, it is far simpler to accept them than to define and explain them; and for lack of further evidence, their case rests. I keep an open and clear understanding of their functions. Above all, I do not *intellectualize* them, lest by doing so I shut out the perceptions that stem from the mysterious universal areas of knowledge that lie beyond myself and beyond all the present capacities of human understanding.

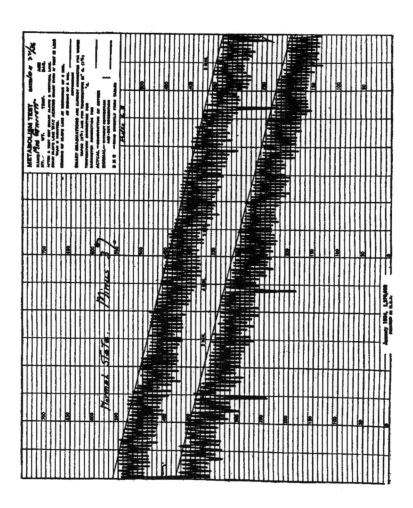

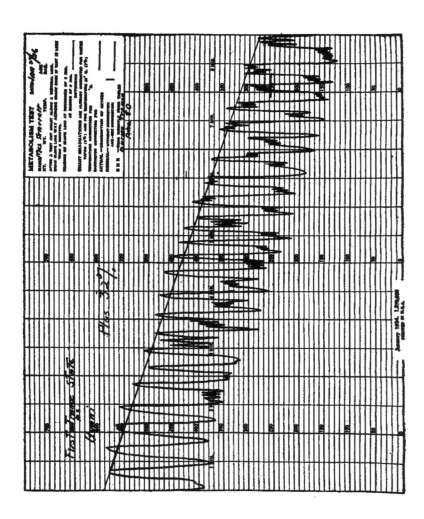

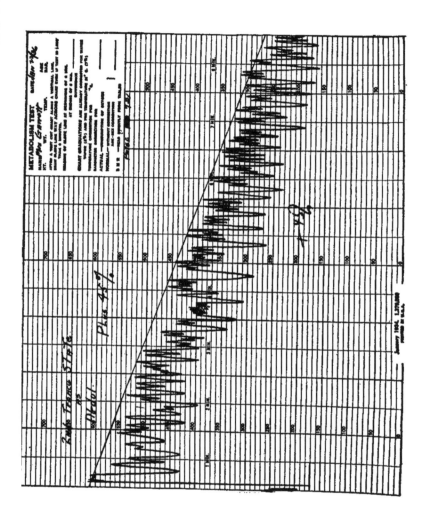

XII
Conclusion

IN THE CHAPTERS of this book I have discussed several aspects of the relations that exist and operate between various types of human perception and awareness and the environing world in which we live—a world in which we reveal and express ourselves only in crude and partial ways. I have emphasized the fact that large phases of our daily living occur in areas which are not dependent on any direct play of sensory perception, but which, on the contrary, occur by means that must remain simply mysterious to anyone who examines them from a rigid sensory basis.

Yet these non-sensory perceptions do, in fact, occur and are completely realistic, and they have been more or less in evidence at all times, down the known ages of man's past. They are not a fresh or new phase in human psychology, but have been present as capacities of the human psyche from time immemorial. But man has always been afraid of is environment; and though he has now conquered countless aspects of the physical elements, he has done so by successively accepting and following the discoveries and revelations of a few pioneers. Through the pioneers, man has never been without a sense of his creative horizon, and he is not without it today. Since he now has in his hand the tools for achieving solutions of all the problems which his physical environment may present, he faces the evolutionary necessity of at last discovering himself.

The capacities in man which operate independently of his sensory faculties are commonly called "psychic," to indicate their non-physical and non-sensory quality. But the real significance of the word "psyche" leads us beyond this superficial differentiation of terms, and probes the very depths of our human nature. "Psyche" is the Greek word for the soul, and the dictionary says that psychology is "the science of the human soul; specifically, the systematic or scientific knowledge of the powers and functions of the human soul, so far as they are known by consciousness." Soul is itself defined as "the spiritual, rational, and immortal part in man; that part of man which enables him to think, and which renders him a subject of moral government …"

In our psychic undertakings, therefore, we are evidently exercising the capacities and qualities of the soul. But we must not become dogmatic here, because the areas of soul-consciousness are undoubtedly far more free and unlimited than those areas of consciousness which our rational minds may reach. What we are probably now discovering —or rediscovering—are the first fringes of an anciently existing evolutionary field which mankind may, or may not, be ready to explore. To me, it seems that the time for this exploration has come; but the issue of course depends upon the actual quality of the world-consciousness as a whole.

We may note, in any case, that one of the outstanding facts about supersensory states of consciousness is that they transcend one's ordinary personal prejudices and predilections. One enters an atmosphere of complete impersonality, beyond the usual need to criticize, analyze, and evaluate. Poised, alert, and concentrated above the personality level, one apprehends the lines of light, the symbols and forms, the sounds and scents that dawn and flash and fade in that nameless place. And for myself I know that between these sequences of psychic "events" and the superpersonal phases of consciousness in which they are perceived, there exists some natural affinity and correspondence of qualities. As we become aware, page by page, of the contents of the novel we read, and come to know from the symbols of its printed words its people, places, and events (which never did exist in physical substance or time), so in supersensory states one perceives, through a different set of symbols, the verities of another state of being. Instead of using my eyes and a telescope to examine a distant planet, I use the breath to transpose my capacities of perception from one level of consciousness to another.

There is a general tendency to make a mystery of this process, which seems to me to be a perfectly natural human operation, and which requires no more talent or training than many other human activities. This tendency is due, I am sure, to the fact that most people refuse or fail to experiment with supersensory types of experience. Yet these are but the reverse of the constant practice of our daily living, in which we transform supersensory ideas into physical form and action ...

Within myself—mentally, emotionally, imaginatively—I decide to go to Washington. There is no positive reason why I should go to Washington, except my own inner wish and inclination to do so. But I decide to go to Washington; and that immaterial decision is the root, the model, the cause, in relation to which countless things in the physical world will have to come into play—time and trains, hotel apartments, restaurants, the personnel of various establishments and the mechanisms of numerous organizations. This is the process by which all of the factual events in our world come into existence and activity.

Is it a monstrous idea that, turning away from time and trains, hotels and the personnel of organizations—from the whole physical world—I can center my consciousness within itself and discover that other side of life, in which my decision to go to Washington originated? To me, the idea of being moved about by forces that I could not discover and know and experience would be a monstrous idea, because—for one thing—to accept such a concept and such an attitude would be to suppose and concede that a cleavage, a breach, exists in the circular play of energy in the universe, and I know there is no such breach. Science knows that nature abhors a vacuum, and does not itself believe in a vacuum. Nor do I. The universe is continuous with the stuff of life, and where there is life there is consciousness.

It is also well known to science, as well as to religion, that the process of the continuity of the universe is based in a trinitarian pattern of the one, the other, and the relation between them—endlessly repeated. Nothing lives to itself alone, and all that exists is united, from the periphery to the center of this global universe. The Christian teaching of the Trinity—three Persons in one God—has its Eastern and theosophical correspondences in a similar trinitarian causal pattern whose parts may be thought of as energy, quality, and manifestation; and these primary models are reflected in the life-force, the nature, and the form of every created thing.

Like everything else, man is constructed on this trinitarian model—spirit, soul, and body. Modern science, in spite of the fact that psychology has set itself up as a science, will have little or nothing to do with ideas of soul and spirit, but confines itself to the field of the physical. It may, however, go so far as to concede that the human constitution might be divided into three broad phases, if one chose so to divide it—the obvious mental, emotional, and physical aspects of the human being. Such a conception of the nature of man limits humanity unwarrantably, as religion believes, for the hope of human salvation lies not in man's physical, emotional, and mental faculties as such, but precisely in the higher capacities of the soul and the spirit that are in him.

If we put aside our prejudices for a moment—whether these be religious or scientific—and consider this problem afresh and quite objectively, remembering meanwhile that in psychology as in physics action and reaction are equal, we shall have to recognize that it is in neither our physical nor our sensory capacities that the decisions of our lives are made, but in the mysterious qualitative phases of our immaterial "nature" or "character." It is in the synthetic areas of human life which, for the present, lie beyond analysis, that our affinities and our aversions are determined and recognized.

We are "electric" all through with the magnetism of life and relationships which, at the physical level, give the atom unsubstantial form as a magnetic field of inter-related electric energies, positive and negative, to equilibrium and in motion. Everything in the world partakes of this atomic dualism. But behind the atom's dual nature there lie that state and moment of creation in which the essence of the universal becomes diffused into individualities, and in which, anon, the essences of individualities are again transmuted into the undifferentiated unity of the whole.

To begin to realize this process is to begin to be universal-minded, soul-conscious; and its outstanding psychological effect is that one begins, through understanding, to lose one's fear of both of those phases of being which we call life and death.

This somewhat metaphysical excursion has definitely to do with our theme, for the human soul may be thought of as that principle in human nature which at once divides and unites the part and the whole, the individual and the universe. By way of the soul, the universal spirit continually animates the individual man; and by way of the soul, the individual, in the practice of aspiration, devotion, love, and worship—activities in which he transcends his individualized separateness—reunites himself, in varying measures, with the whole.

Is supersensory perception religious in its character, then?

In a certain sense, I believe it is. If *religion* means "to bind back to the source," the capacity for perception beyond the physical reach of the senses is a phase in the process of that return. It is to be noted that such "psychic" exercises are in themselves without dogma or any sectarianism. They belong to the great body of natural religion, in which all the sustained but changing processes of nature are continuously involved. Whether or not we believe that as a whole our universe is evolving, we know beyond question that there are vast areas open to the evolution of the individual life. Actually, this is all that any one of us needs to realize. From the point of that realization, we can proceed with our own development, if we will. And I have no doubt that at some stage in our progress we shall experience capacities of perception which transcend the sensory field—just as I am quite sure that the general capacity of the human mind for intelligence, knowledge, and understanding has been definitely advanced and developed in the last three hundred years.

I make bold to write in terms of the soul and the spirit because I am deeply impressed by the conviction that modern human life suffers from a habitual ignoring of horizons. The horizons are there, but we will not look at them. Yet it is in the areas that lie between us and the horizons that man can find—is destined to find—his future development and his fuller freedom. It is not without sympathy and understanding that one urges one's fellow-creatures to lift their eyes and their consciousness from the immediate ring of their personality perceptions; our education in the minute has been long, and the conditions that inhibit our fuller freedom are tense. Yet the Spirit has never been without its witnesses among men; and as I have already said, I believe that the time for a definite expansion of human awareness, through a renewed perception of spiritual horizons, has come.

It should perhaps be emphasized that in considering the theme of super-sensory perception one is dealing with something that is no more mysterious than the other metabolic and thought processes of one's daily living. Very few of us know how the food we eat is secretly transformed into the activities of a world-wide war, a philanthropic enterprise, or a musical composition. We live through these secret processes daily without being aware of them, yet we can become aware of them in some measure by directing the attention of our consciousness to them.

Similarly, the energies of the soul and the spirit in man are constantly being transmuted by the internal processes of our lives into the conscious acceptance or denial of morals and the conditions of the good life. From our present point of view, the soul is the signet of man's alliance with the universal, and movement in this direction is positive and expansive activity. For the acceptance of the idea of the universal, one does not need to deny anything—except his own self-imposed limitations. For instance, we may continue to be as firmly founded in materialism as we choose; we still have to find the secret of substance that lies hidden beyond the atom, whether this atom be the atom of physical substance or the human being considered as an atom in the universe; and it is noteworthy that, in these present times, many of the scientists are expressing their own concepts of the unity of life, their own superpersonal intuitions and inspirations, in purely philosophical terms and in terms of mathematical symbolism. Meanwhile, the political leadership of the world is pressing the general consciousness of mankind toward a wider morality. And though these activities of science and politics are firmly based on materialistic foundations, we can see in them, very clearly, how the human consciousness is moving into the universalistic field.

Though the substance of this chapter is concerned with the return of the individualized consciousness to its source in the universal, the chapter is not intended to be a religious preachment. It is "holy" only in the sense that it speaks of our innate affinity with the whole, the universal Unity. It is "sacred" only in the sense that, in a decidedly profane and confused world, it emphasizes the free nature of the life and consciousness that are in us.

I am convinced that humanity's release from many of its present distresses is to be achieved through a clearer, a more realistic, understanding of the unity existing between the subjective and objective aspects of human life. This conviction, as I have endeavored to show by outlining my own difficulties and developments, is not a theory, but the result of direct experimentation with life. Naturally, I do not mean to urge anyone to undertake the development of his "psychic" powers, but I do urge many to a serious consideration of those inner faculties which operate beyond the fields of sensory perception and beyond the restricted areas of their own personal interests.

Specifically, I wish to emphasize the fact that what we now speak of as the "psychic" phases of our human experience are not abnormal, but normal. Never before has civilized life been so abnormal as now, never before has man's relation to nature been so tenuous and remote. Having become enamored of our own form, reflected in the pool of our man-made civilized world, we are nostalgic with self-admiration, and like Narcissus, we are sinking into this pool of materialism, which will smother the breath of life out of us and leave only a sad memory of a potential excellence that might actually have been.

Any good psychiatrist can explain to you the abnormal and limiting effects of narcissism. Egotism, turned in upon itself, creates a psychological delusion, and the realities of life in the world at large dawn and fade with no more significance than mirages. Action and motive become centered in the self, and the true potentialities of outer relationship are ignored. Are not these the symptoms of humanity's present malaise? East and West, we are viewing racial egotism separating itself from human life and elevating its own obsessions to the dignity of all-that-matters. East and West, we have seen the nations fumbling to preserve their own illusional safety in the midst of a chaos that was the only reality. In these present times especially, it is not the expansive inclusiveness of the psyche that is abnormal but our ignoring of the whole world of realities that lies outside our immediate obsessive concentrations.

It is not without due cause that humanity carries a constant, tremulous, inner hope and fear concerning its own immortality. Establishing the conviction of immortality in our consciousness is the whole aim and business of religion and the fountain of perpetual youth for which science searches. Seeking the illusive mate of his mortality, man has combed the heavens and the earth, without success. But there is an ancient legend which tells that at a council of the gods, when they were considering where they should hide the golden key to man's destiny, so that he should not find it too easily—and so become godlike—they hit upon the clever idea of hiding it where man would be least likely to look for it—deep within himself. And there it has remained hidden throughout the ages and down to the present time.

But now the time for its discovery has come. Disappointed in his long search in the objective realms of existence, and distressed by the repeated failure of his own creations to fulfill the need of his life, man is turning back upon himself and catching glimpses of his own inner nature. He has caught an intuitive flash of insight revealing that this is the way. And though he is slow to turn from all the marvelous achievements of the past, he can never escape from the effects of that mystical moment of psychic perception.

Actually, we do not have to turn away from anything real. We are rooted in the physical world and could not abandon it if we would. Even beyond death, form exists, implying some type of substantiality. What we have to turn away from is our obsession with minutia, our illusion of the importance of parts. We must focus awareness in an ever-evolving perception of synthetic wholes, and progressively set our natures free through the out-ward expanding play of experience, sympathy, and understanding. For the pioneers in life this was once a wild, rough, unknown country; but they have left us maps and memoranda (symbols) which—if we will use them—will lead us smoothly to a new psychological peak in Darien.

Afterword

After Rereading *Awareness*

Having read *Awareness* a second time after so many years have passed, it is easy to see why all of Eileen Garrett's writings appealed to me. There are two major factors involved.

First, she uses the first-person narrative approach that I have recommended to parapsychologists (White, 2000). Even more importantly, this book and most of her other writings tend to present ideas and opinions based on her own exceptional (anomalous and nonordinary) experiences of the psychic and mediumistic type. Such experiences only become what I call *exceptional human experiences* (EHEs) when the experiencers are able to discern their import and meaning and incorporate it their lives in such a way that they realize more of their human potential.

Eileen Garrett had a penetrating analytical mind as well as her intuitive, mediumistic, psychic forms of awareness, and she used it not only to obtain information but to gain understanding. She also was well read and knew many researchers, not only in parapsychology but psychology and psychiatry. This enabled her to understand parapsychology from a unique perspective— from both inside and outside its subject matter.

In effect, she did naturally what I suggest any one do if they have had an exceptional experience that they cannot forget and whose qualities compel them to work with the experience until they understand its meaning. Such meanings often prove to be life-changing in small or large ways. That is when they become *exceptional human experiences*.

In coming up with the EHE idea I was influenced by many people whose ideas I came across in reading countless books and articles and studying many accounts of exceptional experiences. Many of them simply described an experience but did not attempt to discern its meaning. However, often the experiencers mentioned that their experience was "unforgettable" or "one of the most important experiences" of their lives.

What I am suggesting is that whichever class of exceptional experience is being described, whether it be a death-related, psychic, mystical, peak, or nadir experience, simply describing it is only the beginning. I recommend that the experiencer continue to keep it in mind with the aim of becoming aware of its personal, social, global, and vocational meanings, if any.

In rereading *Awareness*, I see that is exactly what Mrs. Garrett did. She describes her experiences and what they taught her about psychic abilities, mediumship, survival, and life itself. Although what she writes was informed by her reading and her many contacts with scholars and scientists, it was always relevant to her personal quest for her vocation and the meaning of her life. In effect, *Awareness* is Mrs. Garrett's EHE autobiography. The latter is a technique I have been developing since the 1990s in which one writes an account of one's life through describing one's exceptional experiences and then trying to potentiate their meanings, primarily in order to increase one's understanding of one's self and one's unique vocation. In effect, this is what Mrs. Garrett did in *Awareness* and other autobiographical writings. Although it took many years for the EHE idea to come to me, often based on the research, ideas, and experiences of many people, Eileen Garrett was one of the important ones.

All these years I have carried with me the realization that what made her writings important was that what she wrote was based on her own personal experience. And her exceptional life experiences were many and varied. I am glad that I read Garrett before I became deeply immersed in the psi experiments that were to consume most of my attention. I have retained a general recollection of her depth of perception and penetrating wisdom, even though in real life she could not always live the way she came across in print. (What human can?) Although my dealings with Eileen Garrett were not frequent, they were never dull. She was certainly an exceptional person. I am grateful to have known her, and for the opportunity to become reacquainted with her through rereading this book.

Awareness would educate and encourage any one who has had one or more exceptional experiences of whatever kind, not necessarily psychic or mediumistic. It is about her personal journey of becoming consciously aware of the world inside and outside her. She was an early explorer of consciousness, including the unconscious, and I think it would be appropriate to say in her case, the supraconscious. Few people have written more penetratingly about what it is like to be psychic, mediumistic, mystic, and human.

Awareness is a memorable record of how Eileen Garrett became aware of her vocation and her deep self, which I think is the primary after-effect and gift of any type of exceptional experience, especially when one works at it in order to penetrate the heights and depths of its meaning and then incorporate it into one's sense of identity, way of life, and worldview.

Rhea A. White
New Bern, North Carolina
November 2006

Eileen J. Garrett
circa 1931
in New York City

Epilogue

So concludes Eileen J. Garrett's *Awareness*. My grandmother's insatiable curiosity for life and how we function continued until her death in 1970 and I suspect continues to this day—in some form—as she tried during her lifetime with dedication to discover.

It is telling that in utilizing her own concepts of *Awareness* she founded the Parapsychology Foundation in 1951 which continues today her quest for the understanding of the psychic components of humankind. She described in her final book. *Many Voices*, published in 1968 that "'on the periphery of sleep' I heard a voice telling me I must get well and build and 'edifice' that would honor the subject (Parapsychology) to which I had devoted my life. I awoke with a feeling of deep conviction that I must begin a new structure containing the best elements of my own work."

I am personally very proud to presently administer the programs of her "edifice" and I welcome people to utilize the resources available at *www.parapsychology.org* and the Eileen J. Garrett Research Library of the Parapsychology Foundation.

I close with a reiteration of one more thought from *Awareness* "… the genius of man consists in the fact that he possesses the searchlight of awareness. And that he is finally learning to understand the unity of the whole field in which it operates."

Lisette Coly
New York City
March 2007

A Selected List of Publications
By and About Eileen J. Garrett

Compiled by Carlos S. Alvarado, Ph.D.

General Biographical Information about Eileen J. Garrett

Angoff, A. (1974). *Eileen Garrett and the world beyond the senses.* New York: William Morrow.

Borgida, L. (1948, January 17). Profile of a publisher. *Los Angeles Times,* n.p.

Eileen J. Garrett, spiritualist, dies. (1970, September 17). *New York Times.*

Hankey, M. W. (1970). Eileen J. Garrett. *Light, 90,* 177–179.

Hastings, A. (2001). The Many Voices of Eileen J. Garrett. *International Journal of Parapsychology, 12*(2), 95–120.

Interview. (1970). *Psychic, 1*(6), 4–6, 32–37.

Rockwell, K. (1949, October 9). Eileen Garrett lives in a world of visions. *The Daily Times Herald* (Dallas), pp. 4,7.

Dingwall, E. J., Angoff, A., & Servadio, E. (1970). Eileen J. Garrett—Recollections of three associates. *Parapsychology Review, 1* (special issue), 2–4.

McMahon, J. D. S. (1994). *Eileen J. Garrett: A woman who made a difference.* New York: Parapsychology Foundation.

Rhine, J. B. (1971). Eileen J. Garrett as I knew her. Journal of the Society for *Psychical Research, 46,* 59–61.

Servadio, E. (1971). Eileen Garrett: A personal recollection. *Journal of the Society for Psychical Research, 46,* 61–64.

Stevenson, I. (1971). Eileen J. Garrett: An appreciation. *Journal of the American Society for Psychical Research, 65,* 336–343.

Books and Articles Written by Eileen J. Garrett

Garrett, E. J. (1939). *My life as a search for the meaning of mediumship.* New York: Oquaga Press.

Garrett, E. J. (1941). *Telepathy: In search of a lost faculty.* New York: Creative Age Press.

Garrett, E. J. (1943). *Awareness.* New York: Creative Age Press.

Garrett, E. J. (1947). A medium's reflections. *Light, 67,* 339–342.

Garrett, E. J. (1949). *Adventures in the supernormal: A personal memoir.* New York: Garrett Publications. (Reprinted with new materials in 2002 by Helix Press.)

Garrett, E. J. (1950). *The sense and nonsense of prophecy.* New York: Creative Age Press.

Garrett, E. J. (1952). The ghost of Ash Manor. *Tomorrow, 1*(1), 50–66.

Garrett, E. J. (1953). The Rockland county ghost. *Tomorrow, 1*(3), 10–23.

Garrett, E. J. (1953). What parapsychology means to me. *Tomorrow, 1*(3), inside front and back covers.

Garrett, E. J. (1953). Psychometry. *Light, 73,* 275–276.

Garrett, E. J. (1954). The aura. Light, 74, 303-306.

Garrett, E.J. (Ed.) (1957). *Beyond the five senses.* Philadelphia: J. B. Lippincott.

Garrett, E. J. (Ed.) (1957). *Does man survive death? A symposium.* New York: Helix Press.

Garrett, E. J. (1957). *Life is the healer.* Philadelphia: Dorrance.

Garrett, E. J. (1961). *Patterns of clairvoyance. Proceedings of two conferenceson-parapsychology and pharmacology* (pp. 14–16). New York: Parapsychology Foundation.

Garrett, E. J. (1963). The nature of my controls. *Tomorrow, 11,* 324–328.

Garrett, E. J. (1968). *Many voices: The autobiography of a medium.* New York: Putnam's.

Garrett, E.J., & Lamarque, A. (1946). *Man—The maker: A pictorial record of man's inventiveness.* New York: Creative Age Press.

Lyttle, J. (1942). *Today the sun rises.* New York: Creative Age Press.

Lyttle, J. (1943). *You are France, Lisette.* New York: Creative Age Press.

Lyttle, J. (1944). *Sheila Lacy.* New York: Creative Age Press.

Lyttle, J. (1961). *Threads of destiny.* New York: Dorrance.

Research with Eileen J. Garrett

Birge, W. R., & Rhine, J. B. (1942). Unusual types of persons tested for ESP. I. A professional medium. *Journal of Parapsychology, 6,* 85–94.

A book-test at a distance of 8,000 miles. (1932). *Psychic Science, 11,* 67–69.

Book tests through Mrs. Garrett. (1926). *Psychic Science, 5,* 210–213.

Carington, W. (1934). The quantitative study of trance personalities. I. Preliminary studies: Mrs. Garrett, Rudi Schneider, Mrs. Leonard. *Proceedings of the Society for Psychical Research, 42,* 173–240.

Carington, W. (1935). The quantitative study of trance personalities. II. Improvements in analysis. *Proceedings of the Society for Psychical Research, 43,* 319–361.

Carington, W. (1939). The quantitative study of trance personalities. New series, I. Revision and extension of the inter-medium experiment. *Proceedings of the Society for Psychical Research, 45,* 223–251.

Carrington, H. (ca. 1933). An instrumental test of the independence of a spirit control. *Bulletin I, American Psychical Institute,* 8–95.

Evans, G. C., & Osborn, E. (1952). An experiment in the electroencephalography of mediumistic trance. *Journal of the Society for Psychical Research, 36,* 588–596.

Goldney, K. M., & Soal, S. G. (1938). Report on a series of experiments with Mrs. Eileen Garrett. *Proceedings of the Society for Psychical Research, 45,* 43–87.

Healy, J. (1984). The happy princess: Psychological profile of a psychic. *Journal of the Society for Psychical Research, 52,* 289–296.

Herbert, C. V. C. (1937). An experiment with Mrs. Garrett. *Journal of the Society for Psychical Research, 30,* 99–101.

Hinchliffe, E. (1930). *The return of Captain W. G. R. Hinchliffe.* London: Psychic Press.

LeShan, L. (1968). A "spontaneous" psychometry experiment with Mrs. E. J. Garrett. *Journal of the Society for Psychical Research, 44,* 14–19.

LeShan, L. (1968). The vanished man: A psychometry experiment with Mrs. E.J. Garrett. *Journal of the American Society for Psychical Research, 62,* 46–62.

LeShan, L. (1995). When is Uvani? *Journal of the American Society for Psychical Research, 89,* 165–175.

McKenzie, J. H. (1929). Investigation of a psychically disturbed house. *Psychic Science, 8,* 103–108.

Pratt, J. G. (1936). Towards a method of evaluating mediumistic material. *Bulletin 23, Boston Society for Psychic Research,* 5–53.

Price, H. (1931). The R-101 disaster (case record): Mediumship of Mrs. Garrett. *Psychic Research: Journal of the American Society for Psychical Research, 25,* 268–279.

Progoff, I. (1964). The image of an oracle: A report of research into the mediumship of Eileen J. Garrett. New York: Garrett Publications.

Puharich, A. (1962). Beyond telepathy. Garden City, NY: Doubleday.

Puharich, H. K. (1966). Electrical field reinforcement of ESP. *International Journal of Neuropsychiatry, 2,* 474–486. (Reprinted in *International Journal of Parapsychology, 9*[4], 175–183.)

A remarkable book-test. (1931). *Psychic Science, 10,* 203–204.

Rhine, J. B. (1934). Telepathy and clairvoyance in the normal and trance states of a medium. *Character and Personality, 3,* 91–111.

Thomas, J. F. (1929). *Case studies bearing upon survival.* Boston: Boston Society for Psychic Research.

Thomas, J. F. (1937). *Beyond normal cognition: An evaluative and methodological study of the mental content of certain trance phenomena.* Boston: Boston Society for Psychic Research.

Ullman, M., & Krippner, S. (1970). Experimental sessions with Mrs. Garrett. In M. Ullman & S. Krippner, *Dream studies and telepathy: An experimental approach* (pp. 32–39). New York: Parapsychology Foundation.

Walker, N. (1929). The Tony Burman case. *Proceedings of the Society for Psychical Research, 39,* 1–46.

Index

Superconscious and, 7
Symbolic images and, 86–93
Trance phenomena and, 108, 109
See Awareness, Consciousness, Psychic
experiences
Survival after death: 69–83
Symbolism: 41, 42, 46, 47, 48–50, 55, 85–
98, 110, 120, 151, 153
Definition of, 85–86
Healing and, 59–60
Trance phenomena and, 135

Tai I Chin Hua Tsung Chih: 139
Telepathy: 1, 9, 10, 11, 19, 66, 69, 92, 104,
108–109, 126, 139
Breathing control and, 46
Cases of, 19–21
"Faith" and, 29, 131
Theosophy: 113, 137
Thought:
Energy and, 10
Reflective form of, 110
Thoughts Through Space (Sherman): 11n,
48, 138
Time: 2
Tomorrow Magazine: vii
Trance: 1, 7, 9, 34, 66, 69, 105–107, 108,
125–142
Altered states and, 125
Definition of, 125–126
Possession and, 125, 127, 127–128
See also Mediumship
Trefoil, the. *See* Garrett, Eileen J., Personal
symbology and
Trinity, the. *See* Christian symbols
Truth, concept of: 142

United Kingdom. *See* Great Britain
United States: xvii, 8, 63, 141
Universities: Duke University, Oxford Uni-
versity, University of Utrecht
University of Utrecht: xvii
Uvani: 106, 107, 108, 109, 134, 138, 139,
141, 144
Biography of, 129–130
See also Mediumship, "controls in";
Garrett, Eileen J., trance phenom-
ena and; Uvani

Visions: xii
Vital "synthetic essence": 71, 72, 73

Waking states of consciousness, psychic
phenomena and: 21
Washington, D.C.: 48, 148, 149
Western mysticism: 51–52
White, Rhea A.: vii, 160
Foreword by, ix–x
Afterword by, 159–160
Wilhelm, Richard: 51
Wilkins, Hubert (Sir): 11n
Long-distance experiment with Sher-
man and, 11–13
World of Dreams (Ellis): 16n
World War I: 135
World War II: viii, xi, xvii, 71, 101–102, 135

Yew tree. *See* Garrett, Eileen J., Personal
symbology and